THE
OMEGA-3
Breakthrough

THE OMEGA-3 Breakthrough

The Revolutionary, Medically-Proven FISH OIL DIET

INCLUDING MENU PLANS & RECIPES

JULIUS FAST

DEVELOPED BY
THE PHILIP LIEF GROUP, INC.

The Body Press
Tucson, Arizona

Special thanks to
Samuel Mitnick

Also thanks to: Gene Brown, Jordan Brown, Joe
Freedman, Anne Halpin, Constance Jones, Sue Katz,
Sharon Kinsky, Genie Leftwich, Philip Lief, Bob
Markel, Andrew Miller, Kevin Osborn,
Peg Parkinson, and Joe Pheifer

THE BODY PRESS
A division of HPBooks, Inc.

575 East River Road
Tucson, Arizona 85704

Manufactured in the United States of America

Book design by The Sarabande Press

Library of Congress Cataloging-in-Publication-Data
Fast, Julius, 1918–
The Omega-3 breakthrough.
Bibliography: p.
1. Omega-3 fatty acids—Therapeutic use.
2. Omega-3 fatty acids—Physiological effect.
3. Fish in human nutrition. 4. Fish as food.
I. Title II. Title: Omega—three breakthrough.
RM666.O45F37 1987   615'.36 . 87–11604
ISBN 0–89586–625–0

10 9 8 7 6 5 4 3 2 1
First Printing

Contents

Contents

THE
OMEGA-3
Breakthrough

⤙ *Part I* ⤚

THE OMEGA-3 BREAKTHROUGH

Saved By A Balloon

One month after I started writing this book on the effects of omega-3 polyunsaturated fats, I was admitted to Yale-New Haven Hospital for a coronary angioplasty. One of my heart's arteries had an obstruction that would inevitably lead to a heart attack, so my doctor decided to remove it.

It all started on a clear autumn morning when I was jogging around the new quarter-mile track in the small Connecticut town where I live. I had a dull feeling in my left arm, a weariness that was not quite pain and yet caused a definite discomfort.

I had gone barely a quarter of a mile, and my impulse was to run through it. Slogans like "no pain, no gain" went through my mind. But the feeling didn't go away, and after three miles I returned to my car and drove home uneasily.

At first, I didn't say anything to my wife, Barbara, about the pain that morning. The discomfort had disappeared when I stopped running, and it seemed too petty to bother about. But the next day, at the track, it returned. This time I cut my run short. I began to feel anxious about it, and the anxiety had a dark edge of fear. This was no cramp or muscle ache. It came on with exertion, and went away when I stopped.

"Now don't worry," I told Barbara at dinner that night, "but I think there's something going on with my heart."

"Your heart!" She stared at me, startled. "What do you mean?"

I told her about the ache in my arm. "It's hard to describe. I don't think it's angina—or what I've always thought angina was like."

"But what's angina like?" Barbara frowned.

"It should be a crushing pain in the chest, but this is in my left arm, and it's hardly a pain—or even an ache. It's more like—well, weariness."

"I think you should call Jon Alexander at once!" she said adamantly. "It's not something to fool around with. Call him now at home!"

Dr. Jonathan Alexander, a good friend, is a cardiologist, and the director of the Cardiac Rehabilitation Program at Danbury Hospital in Connecticut, and an associate clinical professor of medicine at Yale University School of Medicine.

"I hate to bother him this late," I said. "I'll wait until tomorrow."

That wait was terrible for both of us. Acknowledging that it could be my heart opened up a Pandora's Box of horrors with very little hope at the bottom. "I don't understand it," my wife said in bed that night when we both admitted that sleep was impossible. "You've always been in perfect health. You don't smoke. You never get colds, and you've never even been in the hospital."

"I know, I don't understand it either. I've been jogging for twenty years now. My weight is pretty good, too. I'm maybe fifteen pounds overweight, but that's really not much at my height."

I found it hard to accept that I might have a heart condition. Why should this happen to me? I had been a medical writer for many years, but not in the field of cardiology. I am in my 60s and I live a pretty regular life without much stress. I certainly am not Type-A, that compulsive, hard-driven personality that is so prone to heart trouble. I watch my diet and for the past few years I have cut down on red meat and have avoided cholesterol-rich foods—and that hasn't been easy. Like many American men, I take a physical examination every two years and have always been assured that my health was good.

Then again, I have always been an ice cream freak. Indeed, I have driven twenty miles just to sample a new home-made ice cream purported to be richer than any I ever tried before. I also love cheese, and delight in those pre-dinner hors d'oeuvres at friends' houses where the tastiest cheese can be "snarfed" down with drinks.

I called Dr. Alexander at nine the next morning and told him what happened. "I can't believe it's angina," I finished apologetically. "I hate to bother you, but . . ."

"It does sound as if it's related to your heart," he replied, "and that's something we don't fool around with!" He told me to come directly to the hospital.

After an argument about who would do the driving, Barbara drove us over to Danbury Hospital. A nurse took me up to cardiology for the stress test. She shaved parts of my chest and attached electrodes to my skin with suction cups. An electrocardiograph produced a tracing of my heartbeats (an electrocardiogram) as I walked along a treadmill at an increasing pace and an increasing uphill slant.

As I exerted myself, the ache in my arm returned, and the electrocardiogram showed changes in my heartbeat.

Immediately, the nurse injected a radioactive substance into my vein, and disconnected me from the machine. I walked down to the nuclear medicine department where technicians took pictures of my heart.

As Dr. Alexander had expected they would, the pictures showed that one area of my heart muscle was not receiving enough blood.

"There is probably some blockage in a coronary artery," he told Barbara and me as we sat in his office after the tests. "We don't know how much, or just where, but there are many options open. The simplest one is medical management. We'll try to find a drug that will deliver more blood to the heart muscle, or one that will lower the heart muscle's need for oxygen. At this point it looks as if your angina is stable and can be controlled."

"But what if that doesn't work?" I asked.

"Well, there are other possibilities, but let's not go into them until we've checked this one out."

"What about bypass surgery?" I asked. "Would that be one of the options?"

"Of course there is always the possibility that we might consider that," he said.

"Just what is bypass surgery?" Barbara asked.

"It's an operation in which part of the saphenous vein is removed from the leg. The vein is then grafted onto the arteries that supply the heart with blood, to bypass the blocked area," Dr. Alexander explained. "But first let's see just what we're dealing with."

Dr. Alexander gave me nitroglycerin tablets to take whenever the angina came on. They relieved the pain, but after a few days the angina began to occur more frequently. At first it had happened only when I exerted myself, but now it occurred even when I was resting. Finally, one night the pain woke me from a troubled sleep.

I called Dr. Alexander the next morning, and he said, "Get right over here. I want to admit you to the hospital and do an angiogram to see what's going on." A few hours later I was in Danbury Hospital intensive care unit.

An angiogram is a remarkable test. The doctor inserts a catheter—a narrow flexible tube—through a quarter-inch slit in the groin, into an artery and up into the heart. Then the doctor injects radiopaque dye, a dye that x-rays will not penetrate, into the catheter, and the blood vessels around the heart are x-rayed as the blood passes through them.

I remained awake during the painless procedure. I watched a small video monitor, and could see the blockage. I learned that a major coronary artery was blocked in ninety percent of its diameter by a plaque of cholesterol!

"But what I felt in my arm," I asked Dr. Alexander later, "was that angina? It seemed so atypical."

"Angina is usually chest pain, but it can show up as arm discomfort or pain, or even as an ache in the bones of the jaw. The point is," Dr. Alexander stressed, "you're in a very lucky group of patients that can be helped by a new procedure called coronary angioplasty."

Coronary angioplasty, he explained, is very similar to angiography, the procedure I had just had. But in angioplasty, a small, deflated balloon-like tip at the end of the catheter is introduced into the narrowed artery and then inflated. This breaks up the plaque of cholesterol and pushes it against the wall of the artery, unblocking the passage and permitting blood to flow through it, thus reducing the risk of a heart attack.

As I lay hooked up to the monitor in my hospital room, it became evident that the anginal pain I felt in my arm was related to changes in my heart. This thing was progressing too quickly for my peace of mind. At any moment the coronary artery could close completely, and I could have a heart attack. "You're fortunate," Dr. Alexander assured me, "in knowing your own body well enough to realize something was wrong. Too many people ignore something like this until it's too late. Now I think we should get this coronary angioplasty done as soon as possible."

Danbury Hospital is not authorized to do angioplasty, so I went by ambulance to Yale-New Haven Hospital. The ride was smooth enough, but a severe bout of angina hit me halfway through the trip.

The resident accompanying me in the ambulance gave me a nitro-glycerin tablet, which eased the pain after a few minutes.

At Yale-New Haven Hospital I was admitted to the intensive care unit, where the coronary angioplasty would be performed. The pre-surgery consent slip I was asked to sign pointed out a number of possible dire side effects. There was a slight chance of heart attack during the procedure. If the angioplasty was unsuccessful, I might need bypass surgery.

"We will, of course, have an operating team standing by for any emergency," Dr. Henry Cabin assured me. Dr. Cabin, who was to perform the procedure, is a clinical associate professor of medicine at Yale University School of Medicine. "If we need to do a bypass," he continued, "we'll wheel you right into the next-door operating room. The chances of anything going wrong are very slim, but we're prepared."

I had taken the same chances when I had the stress test and the angiogram, so I signed the consent slip willingly. The odds were hugely in my favor.

The procedure took place in a darkened room. Though I was tranquilized, I remained conscious. Sophisticated instruments and technicians' heads blocked my view of the video monitors overhead. The operation, relatively simple and painless, began with the doctor making incisions in my groin and inserting catheters into a vein and an artery. Dr. Cabin easily located and entered the coronary artery, dilating it a number of times with the balloon. After the procedure, I was wheeled back to my bed, and the doctor told me that the operation had been a complete success.

"A very good job," Dr. Cabin assured me. "The artery should stay open. In a very small percentage of cases it closes up in the first twenty-four hours. We'll keep you in intensive care, and if it closes we'll go in again. After the second procedure it always stays open."

All went well over the next twenty-four hours, and I was discharged in a couple of days. Coronary angioplasty is extraordinary because, unlike bypass surgery, there is no traumatic invasion of the body. I had only a few quarter-inch scars at the top of my leg.

Although reassured and ecstatic that the procedure had worked, I was nevertheless apprehensive that the artery might begin to close again. And if it did, how would I know? Not long after returning home

I felt a recurrence of the anginal pain. Certain that my artery was closing again, I nervously called Dr. Alexander. He spent half an hour on the phone reassuring me, and we set a date for another stress test.

A few days later the second stress test showed that the procedure had in fact gone perfectly. The part of my heart that had been deprived of blood was now getting an adequate supply.

"You can do whatever you want," Dr. Alexander said. "Start jogging again, anything. But build up slowly, because you've been hospitalized, and just being in bed for seven days weakens you. However, as far as your heart is concerned, you're home free. That cholesterol level of yours, however . . ."

That cholesterol level of mine! Ten years ago it had been 360 mg, "a high normal," my family doctor had told me. I watched my diet and became more conscientious about jogging. Two years ago my cholesterol level had dropped to 230 mg. My family doctor shrugged. "A high normal, but nothing to worry about." (By the doctor's standards, "normal" seemed to cover a pretty wide range.)

Dr. Alexander had a different idea about my cholesterol level. "Two hundred and thirty is high," he told me after my coronary angioplasty. "Never mind thinking in terms of normal or abnormal. I'd like to see you get your cholesterol below 200. What you went through was caused by the buildup of a plaque of cholesterol in your coronary arteries. That buildup may well have been caused by a very high level of cholesterol in your blood over a number of years."

I thought back to the early days of our marriage, when our three children were growing up. We loved them, and we wanted them to have the best of everything. In the '50s and '60s, the best diet meant "healthy red meat." And that's what we had for dinner four or five times a week: prime cuts, tender and juicy, marbled with fat—and high in cholesterol.

Only later did we learn how that combination of cholesterol and fat could raise the level of cholesterol in the blood. Growing children do need some cholesterol, and everybody needs some fat in their diet, but not as much as we gave them. My thirty-two-year-old son now has a high cholesterol level.

Genetics play a central role in the way people utilize the fats and cholesterol they eat, in whether they excrete it or whether it builds up in their blood and accumulates on the walls of their arteries. Some people can take a diet rich in these substances and still maintain low blood cholesterol. Others reach high levels on a "normal" diet. Your ancestry may well determine your life span.

Evidently, my genetic background made me prone to higher cholesterol levels though less so than many people. Dr. Alexander pointed out to me that "at your age many men with lifetime high cholesterol levels and cholesterol plaques in their coronary arteries face either a heart attack, or, if we intervene in time, a bypass operation involving three or four arteries. You had only one artery severely affected, and we were able to open it without open-heart surgery."

I was lucky. I know that if, ten years ago or even five, I had started eating the right diet instead of all the red meat I did eat, I would have been spared this terrible experience. *Most important*, if I had known then what I know now about omega-3 fish oil, and if I had included omega-3-rich cold-water fish in my diet, I am sure that I would not have experienced the buildup of cholesterol that caused my coronary obstruction.

When I did discover some of the facts about omega-3, I made up my mind to learn everything about it that I could. Was it the miracle substance that so many claimed? Could it prevent coronary artery disease? Was it safe? How much must we take? Does it only help to promote a healthy heart, or does it offer other benefits?

My in-depth research on omega-3 left me with no doubts. It is indeed one of the great discoveries of modern medicine.

◄━ *1* ━►

Clues To A Breakthrough

Fish oil, and the omega-3 it contains, began to come to the attention of medical researchers in the late 1950s. Before that, statistical data had revealed that Americans suffered from a high incidence of heart disease in marked contrast to some ethnic groups in other countries. There were similar contrasts in the statistical incidence of cancer.

Scientists sought clues to explain this disparity. First they looked for leads in the genetic makeup of people with low rates of heart disease and cancer. Was there something in their genes, for instance, that protected them from coronary disease? This approach turned up nothing. Researchers next examined life styles: were the people in these ethnic groups under less strain? This avenue of inquiry also proved to be a dead end.

Gradually, as the studies went on, it became obvious that particularly those ethnic groups with a low incidence of coronary disease—Eskimos, residents of small Japanese fishing villages, people in certain parts of the Netherlands—had one factor in common: a diet plentiful in fish. What was it about fish diets that accounted for the low incidence of disease? The early studies began to unravel the cause.

THE CURIOUS PARADOX
OF THE GREENLAND ESKIMOS

In 1952, Dr. H. M. Sinclair of Oxford University traveled north of the Hudson Bay and Baffin Land in Canada into the bitterly cold, long

Arctic night of the Greenland winter. His goal was to chronicle the eating habits of the Igulik Eskimos. These people struggle on the edge of existence much the same way their ancestors have for centuries. During the Arctic winter, when temperatures drop to -35 degrees Fahrenheit, they subsist on seal blubber and meat. The Igulik consider the cooked contents of the seal stomach a particular delicacy—a fortunate predilection, for this dish provides them with many nutritional elements otherwise missing in their diet. Indeed, they seem to get most of their vitamins from this food. In summer, they supplement their diet with fish, and when possible, caribou.

Dr. Sinclair discovered a paradox: the Igulik Eskimos eat a tremendous amount of fat, but surprisingly, their serum cholesterol levels (the level of cholesterol in their blood) were not unusually high and they suffered virtually no heart disease. Other researchers, who had tested different Eskimo tribes, found these groups to have higher serum cholesterol levels. Yet they too were shown by clinical surveys to have an almost total absence of heart disease.

At first medical scientists thought that Eskimos were genetically protected against heart disease. However, further studies indicated that this was not the case. Hardened arteries and attendant problems were common in these tribes. But the Eskimos of the far north, who lived much as their ancestors and ate a traditional diet, had almost no heart disease.

"The matter," Dr. Sinclair decided, "requires further investigation." Further investigation had to wait for 24 years. In 1976, Dr. Sinclair and two other scientists, Dr. H. O. Bang and Dr. J. Dyerberg, traveled north once again to study the Eskimos of Greenland. They concentrated on the inhabitants of the remote mountainous Umanak region, home of a tribe that had almost no contact with western culture and its dietary habits.

The Eskimos themselves dislike the label "Eskimo" and prefer Innuit, *the people*. Interestingly, though, the word Eskimo translates as "meat eater." Indeed, seal meat and seal blubber (the fat under the skin) make up the bulk of the Umanak diet. The Umanak Eskimos also eat a great deal of salmon, either fresh when the season is right or dried during the rest of the year. Although these north Greenland Eskimos live a hard life, they live to an average age of 60—a longer life span than usual for people living in such difficult conditions.

Dr. Sinclair and his colleagues discovered even more remarkably that only three-and-a-half percent of all deaths among the Umanak Eskimos were due to heart disease. This low level of coronary incidence had not been found among groups of Eskimos who lived in Denmark and who had adopted the Danes' diet. Their rate of heart disease was similar to the Danes.

Again, the only conclusion that Dr. Sinclair and his associates could come to was that the northern Eskimos' diet was what protected them from heart disease. The scientists then proceeded to analyze the food eaten by the Eskimos in northwestern Greenland and compare it with the typical diet eaten by Eskimos living in Denmark. White bread, rice, potatoes and sugar form part of the Umanak Eskimo's everyday diet, but as with the Igulik, fish and seals form the bulk of their meals. One curious fact emerged from Dr. Sinclair's study: the Umanak Eskimos consume almost twice as much cholesterol daily as Eskimos with a Danish diet.

Twice as much cholesterol, but less than half the incidence of heart disease! Were all the studies that linked heart disease to cholesterol in error? Was it possible that excess cholesterol actually *protected* against heart disease? The answers to these questions began to emerge when the researchers analyzed the *types of fat* the Eskimos ate. The Greenland Eskimos ate about half as much saturated fat as the Danish Eskimos. (Saturated fats, such as butter, are solid at room temperature.) They also consumed more polyunsaturated fat (liquid at room temperature).

But the significant difference between the Eskimos' diet and that of the Danes' lay in the varying degrees to which they included two types of polyunsaturated fats. These two fats have confusingly similar names: linoleate and linolenate. Because of its molecular structure, linoleate falls into the omega-6 class of polyunsaturated fats. This omega-6 oil comes from land plants, while linolenate, an omega-3 fat, comes from marine plants. Omega-3 is also found in fish that eat those plants, and in animals that subsist on fish, such as seals.

The traditional Eskimo diet, the researchers discovered, contained a high level of polyunsaturated fats, particularly those of the *linolenic* family: omega-3. By contrast, the Danish diet, like that of most western cultures, included a great deal of saturated fat. Any polyunsaturated fats that it did contain came from terrestrial plants rather than from fish. They were of the omega-6 type, from the linoleic family.

Dr. Sinclair and his colleagues concluded that the composition of Eskimo food "offers a possible way of prophylaxis to people in countries with a high incidence of ischemic heart disease." In other words, Eskimos have something to teach us about a healthy diet.

THE FARMERS OF KYUSHU

Dr. Sinclair's study was not the first to note that eating fish rich in omega-3 appeared to protect people from heart disease. In 1964, a Minnesota researcher had studied another group of fish eaters who led long and healthy lives. Dr. Ancel Keys, director of physiological hygiene at the School of Public Health at the University of Minnesota, teamed up with Dr. Noboru Kimura, director of the Cardiovascular Research Institute at the University of Kurume in Japan. The two researchers set out to study the diet of a group of farmers and fishermen in a typical village in the northern part of the island of Kyushu.

Most of northern Kyushu had become industrialized during World War II, but Keys and Kimura chose to study Tanushimaru, a rural village. The village, although isolated, did not have much arable land, so much of the villagers' diet consisted of what they could catch from the sea.

Drs. Keys and Kimura selected 24 typical men from the village and asked them to stay on their usual diet. The researchers weighed and analyzed everything the men ate. They found not only that the diets of these Japanese men were low in total fats, but that the type of fat they did eat was very different from the fat in western diets.

The men of Tanushimaru consumed an average of about three ounces of fresh or dried fish a day, which supplied one fifth of their total dietary fat. Because fish contains linolenic polyunsaturated fats, composed of omega-3 oils, these Japanese villagers received four times as much omega-3 as people who ate a typical European diet.

The study also found that on the average, the Japanese men had much lower serum cholesterol levels than men in the United States. In addition, Japanese men tended to be much thinner than American men and, most important of all, they had a remarkably low incidence of coronary artery disease. The two scientists also remarked that this group experienced a lower death rate from all causes than there would be in a similar group of men of the same age in the United States.

In the first five years of the study by Drs. Keyes and Kimura, only two deaths in the village of Tanushimaru were due to heart disease. According to statistics, a similar group of men in the United States would experience over 12 such deaths. In the second five years of the study, a total of 57 village men died from all causes, while in an equal number of men of the same age in the United States there would have been about 75 deaths. They concluded that the lower incidence of disease and death among the men of Tanushimaru was directly linked to the high proportion of fish in their diet. Their diet is very similar to that of the rest of Japan.

In addition, the researchers noted that the villagers used *natane*, or rapeseed oil, for much of their cooking. The rape (from the mustard family) is one of the few land plants that manufactures omega-3. Most plants that produce polyunsaturated oils tend to form the linoleic, or omega-6, type, but algae, seaweed, and the plants in plankton form the linolenic, or omega-3, type of polyunsaturated oil.

On land, however, very few species of edible plants contain significant amounts of omega-3. Flax, which yields linseed oil; rape, the source of rapeseed oil; and soybeans and soybean oil each offers a good source of omega-3. Walnut oil also provides some omega-3, while wheat germ oil and butternuts contain smaller amounts. Perilla, or "Beefsteak," an uncommon species of plant from Japan, is supposed to have the highest percentage of omega-3 oils of any land plant, but as yet the plant is not widely available.

Omega-3-rich oils derived from land plants have a number of disadvantages which make them difficult to incorporate into most diets. Linseed oil has five times as much omega-3 as rapeseed oil, but is not very palatable. I have tried cooking and making salad dressing with the kind produced for human consumption, but it tends to taint food with the taste of old paint rags. Though soybeans contain a great deal of omega-3, commercially produced soybean oil does not represent a good source of omega-3. Because linolenic (omega-3) oils oxidize rapidly and spoil easily, soybean oil manufacturers try to decrease the risk of spoilage by removing linolenic acid.

The villagers of Tanushimaru, however, use rapeseed oil for cooking. They cook a popular fried dough cake in the oil, and have a favorite between-meals snack of a kind of French toast fried in rapeseed oil. They also eat rape itself as a vegetable. In the early spring they boil the tender shoots and immature seed heads as potherbs. The researchers found that rapeseed oil counted for one tenth of the average consumption of fats and oils in the village.

The two researchers carried out similar studies on the dietary habits of other Japanese towns, and the nutritional section of the Bureau of Public Health of the Ministry of Health and Welfare in Tokyo instituted a major survey of the entire country. The results of all these studies confirmed those of the research carried out in the village of Tanushimaru. For all of Japan, the daily consumption of fish per person was five times what it was in the United States.

The studies of the Greenland Eskimos and the Japanese fishing village aroused considerable interest in the medical world. Dr. Keys went on to study coronary heart disease in a number of other countries, and found that, in contrast to the residents of western countries, the Japanese had a very low rate of death from the disease. He also found that average daily per capita consumption of fish among the Japanese was about 100 mgs, that is, three and one-half ounces. There are no reliable statistics on how much fish the western world consumes, but it is no doubt much lower in the United States.

Dr. Keys also found that the residents of the island of Okinawa, who ate the most fish, had the lowest death rate. In another study, Dr. Keys compared the eating habits of a Japanese farming village with those of a fishing village. Those who lived in the fishing village, as would be expected, ate three times the amount of fish that the farmers ate—and their death rate from heart disease was far less.

In the '60s, at the time of the studies, most Japanese still ate a traditional diet. But today, all this is changing. As Japan becomes more westernized, ice cream and sugary soft drinks, hot dogs and French fried potatoes, and even pizza have become more common in the diet of the average Japanese citizen.

THE ZUTPHEN STUDY

These studies of the Eskimos and the Japanese, as well as many others, inspired a group of Dutch scientists to carry out further research. Drs. Daan Kromhout, Edward B. Bosschieter and Cor de Lezenne Cou lander had a perfect opportunity at their disposal to investigate the relationship between a diet high in fish and the incidence of heart disease.

Since 1960, other researchers had conducted an ongoing longitudinal study of a group of middle-aged men who had lived in the town of Zutphen in the Netherlands. The study, which investigated the relationship of diet and other factors to the incidence of disease, had been going on for 20 years. A longitudinal study such as this can last throughout the entire lifetime of the participating individuals. This distinguishes it from the more typical cross-sectional study, which examines subjects at one point in their lives and does not include follow-up of more than a few years.

Zutphen, an old industrial town in the eastern part of the Netherlands, had a population of 25,000 when the study began. The researchers chose a random sample of 872 men, 40 to 60 years of age, who had lived in Zutphen for at least five years. They gave all 872 subjects a physical exam and monitored their diets over the years. Since any ongoing record of the diets of all the men in the longitudinal study had been carefully kept, this was a perfect opportunity for the Dutch scientists to see whether those who ate more fish had a lower incidence of coronary heart disease. Would the Dutch study confirm the Greenland findings?

A variety of risk factors has an impact on the occurrence of heart disease, so the researchers noted each of the greatest risk factors the men were subject to during the years of the study. These factors included blood pressure, cholesterol levels, smoking, physical activity, employment background and diet. The researchers found that 20 of the men had some kind of heart disease when the study started. In the 20 years since, 390 men died from various causes. Of these, 78 died of coronary heart disease.

During the same period, the men ate an average of more than one-half ounce of fish each day, about five ounces a week. Lean fish, such as cod and plaice, constituted approximately two thirds of this amount, while only one third was fat fish, such as herring and mackerel, rich in omega-3.

The study revealed an inverse relationship between fish intake and death from coronary heart disease. Men who ate large amounts of fish (about ten ounces a week) were much less likely to have died of coronary heart disease than those who ate little or no fish. The fish eaters, in fact, had less than half the incidence of heart disease.

The Zutphen study also showed that even a small amount of fish might protect against heart attacks. The Greenland Eskimos ate an average of close to a pound of fish per day, and the Japanese fish eaters averaged three and one-half ounces per day, but the men of Zutphen averaged only a little more than half an ounce per day. The researchers concluded that just one or two weekly meals of fish rich in omega-3 polyunsaturated fats might play a valuable part in preventing heart disease.

In another part of the study, when the researchers replaced the typical five and a quarter ounces of cheese eaten every day by the men in the study with seven ounces of mackerel, the participants' serum cholesterol levels went down and they had fewer heart attacks. The cheese that forms a part of the Dutch diet is very high in cholesterol, and omitting it from the diet could have accounted for much of the drop in serum cholesterol levels. But the researchers found that the men who ate a moderate amount of fish and continued eating cheese were also less likely to have clogged arteries, although they did not necessarily have lower cholesterol levels or higher HDL[1] levels. *Thus they were still protected against heart attacks.*

The researchers theorized that omega-3 intake, as well as lowered levels of serum cholesterol, might have contributed to this lower incidence of heart disease. They noted, however, that two thirds of the fish eaten by the men in the study contained only small amounts of omega-3. As a result, they left open the possibility that fish might contain another substance with a beneficial effect on the cardiovascular system. But their observation seemed more likely to support the conclusion that even low levels of omega-3 could have an impact on cholesterol levels and heart disease.

These early studies had identified fish oil as the focus for future research. But no one could have guessed how revolutionary omega-3 would be as a potential preventative agent against man's most painful and killing diseases.

[1] HDL is High Density Lipoprotein, a good cholesterol. The next chapter will explain how HDL reduces the risk of heart disease.

⚓ 2 ⚓

Bad Fats Versus
Good Fats

*C*areful examination of the results of study after study, plus the endorsement of the studies and their implications by the American Medical Association, convinced me that omega-3 can provide many health benefits. My conviction was further reinforced while I recovered from my coronary angioplasty. Each day at Yale-New Haven Hospital, a teaching institution, a bevy of interns accompany doctors on their rounds. Dr. Henry Cabin, who had performed my angioplasty, arrived at my bed one day after the operation, followed by an entourage of students. Instead of inquiring about my health, however, the students greeted me with a veritable barrage of questions about omega-3. "How much fish do you have to eat each day for the fish to have an effect?" "What is the proper dosage of capsules as a substitute for eating fish?"

Dr. Cabin had told them I was writing a book on the topic. They were keenly interested in understanding omega-3's effect on the heart and coronary arteries. Their intense interest convinced me that omega-3 is potentially a tremendously valuable nutritional element. I also realized that it is easier to understand how omega-3 works if you know something about the heart and circulatory system.

PERHAPS MORE THAN YOU WANT TO KNOW
ABOUT THE HEART AND ARTERIES

Recently, we had some plumbing difficulties in our house. The old iron water pipes had to be replaced. They had been in service for over 50 years. "Look at that!" the plumber exclaimed, as he showed me a cross section of pipe he had sawed in half. The inside was so clogged with rust that only a tiny trickle of water could have gotten through. "No wonder you're having trouble!" I was reminded at once of my clogged artery.

A healthy blood vessel is elastic and smooth inside. Blood flows freely through it, and the vessel can expand easily to accommodate increased blood flow. But as we grow older, our arteries, the blood vessels that carry blood away from the heart to the rest of the body, become less flexible. In addition, cholesterol sometimes builds up on the artery walls. Doctors call this condition atherosclerosis, or hardening of the arteries. Atherosclerosis tends to develop at small bruises or breaks in the artery's lining, although not all arterial injuries lead to atherosclerosis.

Injuries to the interior of arteries may result from the normal turbulence of blood rushing past bends in the blood vessel, or they can come from excess force exerted on artery walls by high blood pressure. Other sources of arterial distress include smoking, emotional stress, and genetic predisposition. Once a tear or scratch forms in the artery, white blood cells and platelets arrive to help in the healing process. Sometimes their activities trigger atherosclerosis.

As they work to heal the injury, white blood cells attract cholesterol to the site. Meanwhile, platelets stick together to form a protective covering for the injury while it heals. The cholesterol drawn by the white blood cells tends to deposit on the clot formed by the platelets, and a fatty plaque begins to develop. Platelets forming the clot also release a chemical that causes the muscles of the artery to divide and increase in number, making the blood vessels more rigid. When arteries throughout the body narrow, blood pressure rises and the heart has to work harder to pump blood through them. This causes a strain on the heart and creates excess pressure in smaller blood vessels.

If atherosclerosis occurs in the arteries that feed the heart, the result is coronary artery disease, also termed coronary heart disease, or ischemia ("reduced blood flow"). Because coronary arteries are quite small in diameter, patches of cholesterol can easily build up in them. Atherosclerosis increases the risk of heart attack because the muscles of the heart, which arteries feed, become starved for the oxygen that blood carries. Many other heart conditions can also result.

In other cases, the blood flow may not be restricted enough to cause symptoms. People with a lesser condition may never realize that they have coronary artery disease. Occasionally, small new arteries grow and form collateral circulation around the blockage. If this collateral circulation is strong, ischemia may never occur.

If the heart temporarily fails to get enough blood, pain—angina— results. Angina usually occurs in the chest, and when it does it is labeled angina pectoris. Angina can also occur in the arm or jawbone. Physical exertion, in which the heart works harder, can bring on angina if the heart doesn't receive enough oxygen from the blood. When the body rests or receives only moderate exercise, it is usually free of angina. Angina is the body's warning that the heart needs more oxygen than the coronary arteries can provide.

Stable angina, or stable exertional angina, occurs only during exertion. When it occurs, no real damage takes place, but the danger is nonetheless there. Stable angina can usually be controlled by drugs, a change of life style, or a combination of the two. Angina sufferers try to avoid the excitement and exertion that may bring on attacks.

If an obstacle blocks the coronary artery to the point where the heart is severely deprived of oxygen, a heart attack, or myocardial infarction, can occur. While coronary heart disease doesn't always result in a heart attack, it increases the chances that one will happen. During a heart attack, the part of the heart muscle that is deprived of oxygen ceases to function. Sometimes the damage to the heart is so widespread that heart failure and death occur, but 3 out of every 4 people who have a heart attack survive. Survival depends on the condition of the other coronary arteries and on how much of the heart is affected.

No matter what the poets say, a damaged heart can repair itself. Some people who survive heart attacks recover completely and permanently. Other heart attack victims, however, despite the fact that they continue to lead full lives, run the risk of future attacks. And approximately 1 out of every 2 people who have heart attacks continue to have angina and need ongoing medical treatment.

The best way to prevent heart attacks and angina is to keep blood vessels open and blood pressure down. In part, this amounts to reducing the level of cholesterol and triglycerides (fat molecules) in the blood. High blood cholesterol or triglyceride levels indicate that plaque may be building up in the arteries. As the blood vessels in the body become stiffer and narrower, blood pressure rises. High blood pressure is the most obvious sign that the heart must work harder than it should to circulate blood through the body and that you are in danger of having a heart attack.

Medication can reduce blood pressure, but researchers have not yet developed a drug capable of safely reducing cholesterol levels in the blood (*serum* cholesterol). The few drugs that *do* lower serum cholesterol levels have unpleasant side effects—some of which are even more dangerous than the effects of cholesterol itself.

BAD FATS VERSUS GOOD FATS

Cholesterol, a waxy substance with a pearly appearance, is present in animal fats and oils. Meat, milk and eggs provide cholesterol in varying amounts. Cholesterol plays a vital role in the body, particularly in the development of nerve and brain tissue in very young children. The human liver, kidneys, adrenal glands, brain tissue, nerve fibers, blood and bile each contain some cholesterol. Because the body manufactures most of the cholesterol it needs, much of the cholesterol we consume in our diets only contributes to the risk of heart disease.

Diets low in cholesterol have proven an effective way to lower serum cholesterol. A 1970 study conducted by scientists in 7 countries sought to establish the precise nature of the relationship between diet, cholesterol levels, and the incidence of heart disease. The study revealed a definite link between the elevated serum cholesterol levels of people on high-cholesterol diets and their increased risk of heart attack. It further showed a connection among diets rich in saturated fats (a building block of triglycerides), high cholesterol levels and heart disease. The researchers concluded that eating saturated fats raises the level of cholesterol in the bloodstream, which in turn leads to a greater risk of heart attack.

Triglycerides make up most dietary and body fats and can contribute to heart disease if too many of them are present in the bloodstream. When 3 fatty acid molecules combine with a glycerol molecule (glycerol is a product of the fermentation of sugar) the result is a triglyceride. The way these molecules are formed is crucial to your health. The three types of fatty acids that make up triglycerides—saturated, monounsaturated and polyunsaturated—have very different effects on cardiovascular health.

Fatty acid molecules are chains of carbon atoms linked to hydrogen atoms. If you think of the bonds between atoms as hooks, you can easily envision a saturated fat as a molecule with a hydrogen atom hanging on each of its hooks. A monounsaturated acid has one empty hook, while a polyunsaturated acid has 2 or more empty hooks.

The more highly saturated the fat, the harder it is at room temperature. Butter, for instance, is more saturated than margarine, which in turn is more saturated than vegetable oil. Fish oil, meanwhile, remains liquid even in very cold temperatures. It contains omega-3, a highly polyunsaturated fatty acid. (The oil from all fish contains omega-3, but cold-water fish oil has the greatest concentrations.) Meat, eggs and dairy products all contain saturated fats to one degree or another. Most plant fats (referred to as omega-6 oils), such as corn oil, soybean oil, sunflower oil and safflower oil, are high in polyunsaturates. A few, however—coconut oil, palm oil and cocoa butter—are highly saturated. Fats such as olive and peanut oil fall into the monounsaturated category, and are also grouped with the omega-6 oils. Plant oils offer the additional benefit of having no cholesterol content.

Cholesterol and triglycerides belong to a group of substances known as lipids. Although lipids will not dissolve in water, they can travel through the bloodstream as part of the water-soluble compounds called lipoproteins. Lipoproteins consist of protein, carbohydrates and lipids (such as cholesterol and triglycerides). Depending on the proportion of protein to fat that they contain, lipoproteins fall into two categories: high density lipoprotein (HDL) and low density lipoprotein (LDL). The "good fat" HDL carries cholesterol away from the body tissues to the liver for excretion from the body. The "bad fat" LDL can contribute to the accumulation of cholesterol on arterial walls.

Clearly, HDL and LDL are factors in the probability of contracting heart disease. The percentage of HDL in the blood gives a more accurate reading of the risk of coronary artery disease than can a measure of the cholesterol level. High HDL levels and low LDL levels indicate a reduced likelihood of heart attack. The ratio between the two is as important as the actual level of each. In fact, by dividing total serum cholesterol by HDL cholesterol, a figure of great importance for assessing cardiovascular risk emerges. An average risk factor is 4.5–4.7, with higher numbers (i.e. less HDL per total cholesterol) signifying greater risk.

Diet has a profound effect on the amount of HDL and LDL in the bloodstream. Studies have shown that diets high in polyunsaturated fats and low in saturated fats can lower the level of LDL in the blood, which in turn reduces serum cholesterol and triglycerides. The more highly unsaturated the fat, the better it is for the heart. Saturated fats increase cholesterol levels. For many years, scientists believed that monounsaturated oils had a neutral effect on the body, but recent research has shown that they lower LDL levels much as polyunsaturated fats do. Omega-3, a highly polyunsaturated fat, has the greatest ability of all polyunsaturates to lower cholesterol levels. In addition, omega-3 actually raises the level of HDL in the blood, thus lowering the risk of coronary artery disease even further.

WHAT ARE OMEGA-3 FATTY ACIDS?

At a recent American Heart Association Conference, Dr. Roger Illingworth, associate professor of medicine and biochemistry at Oregon Health Sciences University, defined omega-3 fatty acids as "long-chained metabolic products from linolenic acid." (All cells produce metabolic products in the course of their normal functioning.) "Linolenic acid," Dr. Illingworth explained, "is a fatty acid with 18 carbons and 3 double bonds. It is manufactured exclusively by plants. When animals consume and metabolize plants rich in linolenic acid, they produce omega-3."

Plankton, a minute form of marine life, is part plant and part animal. Its plant component manufactures linolenic acid. Fish eat the plankton, and the linolenic acid breaks down in their bodies into two types of omega-3 fatty acids: EPA (eicosapentaenoic acid) and DHA (docosahexaenoic acid). EPA has 20 carbon atoms with 5 double bonds; DHA has 22 carbons with 6 double bonds. "Omega" in the name omega-3 represents the last letter of the Greek alphabet. The name reflects the chemical structure of the acids, in which the first double bond is located three carbon atoms from the terminal (omega) end of the molecule.

The presence of so many double bonds makes omega-3 highly polyunsaturated, so EPA and DHA are extremely liquid. The liquidity of EPA and DHA serves a vital function in fish, who require body fat that remains fluid even in very cold water.

HOW DOES OMEGA-3 WORK IN THE BODY?

Omega-3 has many health benefits for humans. As a polyunsaturate, it lowers LDL and raises HDL levels, thus reducing serum cholesterol. It also reduces triglyceride levels, and its highly fluid nature appears to impact cholesterol levels further. According to Dr. John S. Parks, assistant professor of comparative medicine at Bowman Gray School of Medicine, Wake Forest University in Winston-Salem, North Carolina, the cholesterol found in laboratory animals fed fish oil has a liquid core. "We are hypothesizing," he remarks, "that the liquidity of the core may make it easier for the cholesterol to get out of the atherosclerotic plaques once they form, so the cholesterol is more easily carried back to the liver where it can be excreted."

Most of omega-3's benefits, however, derive from its effects on platelets. Omega-3 changes the way platelets function, and thus can play a role in relieving conditions related to platelet functioning, such as coagulation and inflammation. Platelets convert fatty acids into prostaglandin, a substance that controls the growth of arterial muscle cells and is crucial to platelet clotting. Typically, the prostaglandin produced by platelets combines with a substance known as arachidonic acid to form thromboxane, which makes platelets sticky. The presence of thromboxane allows platelets to clot, a function vital to healing but potentially dangerous to the heart. If platelets clot too easily, they can contribute to atherosclerosis—and heart attack.

Omega-3 can reduce clotting by inhibiting the production of thromboxane. Arachidonic acid, found in grains and vegetable seeds, usually combines freely with prostaglandin to make thromboxane. The omega-3 fatty acid EPA, however, is similar to arachidonic acid, but it does not convert to thromboxane as easily. EPA interferes with the ability of arachidonic acid to combine with prostaglandin, resulting in reduced production of thromboxane. In this way, EPA decreases platelet stickiness and the tendency of blood to clot.

EPA also accumulates in body tissues, particularly in the cells that line artery walls. Its presence causes the cells to manufacture prostacyclin, a chemical which inhibits platelet clumping. By its dual action on the stickiness of platelets, omega-3 can reduce the likelihood that plaques of cholesterol will develop on the artery walls. And though scientists have not yet figured out exactly how it works, omega-3 further benefits cardiovascular health by lowering blood pressure.

Omega-3's interference with the metabolism of arachidonic acid alters the production not only of thromboxane but of leukotrienes. Leukotrienes aggravate inflammation and alter other immune responses. EPA's role in the production of leukotrienes has proven beneficial to conditions such as arthritis, diabetes, psoriasis, lupus, nephritis and some cancers. Researchers continue their efforts to discover just how far omega-3 can go toward improving human health.

3

The Link Between Omega-3 And Cholesterol

*I*t was a bitterly cold day when I took the express bus up to the Bronx to interview Dr. Judith Wylie-Rosett, assistant professor of medicine at Albert Einstein College of Medicine. Albert Einstein, a great complex of buildings, rears up out of the sprawling urban landscape. Dr. Wylie-Rosett's thirteenth floor office has a northern view, of Westchester and City Island.

Dr. Wylie-Rosett had recently spoken at a seminar of the New York affiliate of the American Heart Association. In her talk on the problems of translating research into clinical practice, she had focused on the benefits of omega-3 fatty acids. She had also described risks in prescribing omega-3 pills to patients. I wanted her to explain her ideas to me, and she agreed to be interviewed.

"There have been a lot of studies on the action of omega-3," she told me, "studies which have explored its tremendous potential. What we need now are randomized, well-controlled clinical studies with placebos. These studies should involve many people. A larger study might answer several questions about the mechanism of action and the proper dosage of omega-3."

"But there have been quite a few studies of large groups of people," I protested.

"Yes, but most of them have been epidemiological studies of populations that either did or did not have omega-3 in their diet: the Greenland Eskimos, the Japanese, and the Dutch. Now it's time to do larger studies. We need to put people with various problems on omega-3 and see how they react."

"In the meantime," I asked, "what do you think of adding fish to the diet?"

She said, "I think it makes sense to eat fish about three times a week, and of course to replace meat with fish. The advantage to that would be the increase in the amount of polyunsaturated fats in your diet. But you realize that three fish meals a week may not benefit someone who is trying to get a true pharmacological effect out of omega-3, the kind that they may need for, say, migraine or arthritis."

"But what about the effects of a fish diet on the average person? Perhaps it would serve a prophylactic purpose."

"It would be an excellent prophylactic. Even beyond the benefits of omega-3 fatty acids, it would replace meat, a source of saturated fat, with fish, a source of polyunsaturated fat."

"Then you say that there is a definite benefit in lowering the amount of saturated fats and cholesterol in the diet. Will this do it?"

"Oh yes. Remember that with the fish, you may not lower the amount of dietary cholesterol—because fish does have cholesterol, although it's a different kind. Even more important, you would lower the saturated fats you take in and replace them with polyunsaturated fats.

"Most studies reported by the American Heart Association have found that if we place a group of people on special diets and modify their life style, we can get a five to ten percent reduction in total cholesterol, assuming they stick to the diet. However, some seem to respond better than others."

"Do you know why?"

"Well, some people may metabolize cholesterol, burn it up in their bodies differently. Most people respond to a low-cholesterol, modified-fat diet with a lowering of their blood cholesterol level. But occasionally you do run across someone whose level of cholesterol won't budge, even if they're on the same diet that gave others a hundred milligram drop. This makes it hard to set realistic expectations for individuals."

She shook her head. "I feel good when I get a dramatic response. Sometimes I'll run up against someone with a 260 or 270 cholesterol level, someone who eats a lot of cheese, two eggs and bacon in the morning, steak for dinner, and I'm almost grateful because I know that with the proper diet I can probably get their level of cholesterol down.

"However, when someone on a good, sensible diet—very little meat and high-fat dairy products and no eggs—comes in with a high cholesterol level, I can't expect much to happen no matter how much I push polyunsaturated oils. They've done all the right things, and nothing seems to help."

"What do you consider a normal cholesterol level?" I asked.

Dr. Wylie-Rosett showed me a chart of cholesterol levels based on the recommendations of a panel of experts on heart disease and cholesterol. The panel was convened by the National Institutes of Health in December of 1984. It defined two categories of high blood cholesterol associated with increased risk of coronary heart disease.

CHOLESTEROL LEVELS
Risks of Coronary Artery Disease by Age

	Moderate Risk	*High Risk*
Age 20 to 29	Greater than 200	Greater than 220
Age 30 to 39	Greater than 220	Greater than 240
Age 40 and over	Greater than 240	Greater than 260

"Family physicians," she remarked, "are just not concerned enough with cholesterol levels. I've had a number of physicians ask me about their patients with cholesterol levels in the 230 to 260 range. They didn't know if those levels were normal, and some medical labs feel that the normal range goes up to 300, or at least 250!"

"I left the hospital after my angioplasty with a cholesterol of 223," I said, studying the chart. "The chart says I'm below the moderate risk for my age."

"That's right."

"But ten years ago I had a cholesterol of 360."

"That would have put you at the very high-risk level. You've moved yourself from high-risk to lower-than-moderate risk."

"Yes, but I think I locked the barn door after the horse was stolen. I did it a little late. On the other hand, I might have been worse off if I hadn't stuck to a reasonably sensible diet for the last ten years. Now I drink skim milk, and I've cut out all eggs and cheese and whatever other cholesterol I can. I eat fish at least three times a week, and I hope to get my cholesterol below 200."

"You seem to be a good responder to a sensible diet."

"Well, I've had a good scare!"

"Now I don't want to give you the idea that some people don't respond at all—it's just a matter of degree. You must remember that for every one percent reduction in total cholesterol, you get a two percent reduction in risk. Assuming someone has a 250 cholesterol and they can reduce it to 225, that's ten percent and that gives them a twenty percent reduction in the risk of coronary heart disease."

I asked Dr. Wylie-Rosett whether someone could have high HDL and low LDL levels, along with a high cholesterol level, and still be at risk. She told me that research had not yet determined the answer to my question. Most doctors won't bother with a test for HDL if a patient has a high cholesterol level. Dr. Wylie-Rosett further noted that people with cholesterol levels between 200 and 300 are the ones who should be most concerned with HDL. She pointed out that while testing for HDL is still an expensive procedure, she felt that the HDL test is useful for determining who should go on a special diet and who should take omega-3 fish oil capsules.

There is a new machine that tests for HDL levels with a simple finger puncture, she explained, and although the machine is expensive, the test itself is inexpensive. Once the machine becomes widely available, schools and health fairs might be able to afford them. That could make population screening much easier and less expensive.

I brought the conversation back to omega-3. Dr. Wylie-Rosett agreed that cholesterol levels in the blood and the action of omega-3 are closely related. I asked about children and omega-3, whether it was a good idea to give the fish oil capsules to children or adolescents.

"I wouldn't. No, it's far better to teach them to eat properly—including fish. I wouldn't give omega-3 supplements to the average child. But if it were a child from a high-risk family, it would be different. If the child has a cholesterol level of 270, and I've done whatever I could with diet—well, I'd recommend testing omega-3 in ten-year-olds under those conditions."

"What about giving them drugs to lower cholesterol?" I asked.

"There are some, like the resins, that are effective, but they are pretty awful to take. They're gritty and they taste like sand. One 23-year-old with high cholesterol, from a high-risk family, told me she hated the drugs so much that she decided to become a vegetarian and to also eat fish. She did that and planned her diet to be high in soluble fibers, and it worked. That diet, vegetables and fish, lowered her cholesterol as much as the drugs would have!"

"What are soluble fibers?"

"The fibers soluble in water include those found in beans, guar gum, pectin, oat bran and barley. There are some interesting studies going on about the effect of these in lowering cholesterol. If we were to recommend a diet to lower cholesterol, the ideal one would include good sources of soluble fiber."

She added that beans of all sorts are high in soluble fibers, and so, theoretically, they should also aid in lowering cholesterol. Different types of beans should be part of any healthy diet. Dr. Wylie-Rosett pointed out that wheat bran didn't do much to lower cholesterol, although it may help prevent colon cancer and regulate the bowels.

The diet best for the heart, she said, would have no meat—or only a modest quantity of lean meat—plenty of vegetables, bran and carbohydrates, and a variety of fish, especially the fatty cold-water fish rich in omega-3.

"What about adding omega-3 capsules to the diet plan?"

"Well, I think we should be careful there," she said. "Capsules with omega-3 are available in health food stores and drug stores, and you don't need a prescription to buy them, but we still have to find out if there is any danger to the public in using them."

"What do you think that danger might be?" I asked.

"For one thing, these capsules contain a fair amount of cholesterol, and for another the fish the oil comes from may have taken in a good deal of environmental contamination. We can deal with the first problem by removing the cholesterol from the capsules. In fact, some companies that produce the capsules advertise that they have done just this. As for the environmental contaminants, unless we know what they are, it's hard to remove them.

"Still another potential source of trouble arises when someone with multiple medical problems takes the capsules. For example, a patient with coronary artery disease may be taking an anticoagulant drug to keep the blood from clotting. If they add a large amount of omega-3 on top of that, it could produce a real problem with bleeding. But of course, one can make the same argument against aspirin.

"You shouldn't take fish oil unless the doctor has specifically recommended it or has discussed it with you. I think it's a matter of public education. People should know more about omega-3 fatty acids and their effects. It's up to the physicians to be more careful in taking histories, and they must also alert patients to the possible dangers.

"One of the big advantages of a cold-water-fish diet over taking omega-3 supplements is in calorie counting," she pointed out. "Oils add calories to the diet. When you substitute fish for meat as part of your diet, you don't increase your calorie count. If you add fish oil capsules to the diet, and still leave in meats and other cholesterol products, you may not do as well. You may get the benefit of the platelet action of omega-3, but you may not get as great a lowering of lipids and cholesterol."

"Now that we're talking of calories, would you say that a lean person has a better chance at cardiovascular fitness?"

Although sure that it was better to be lean, Dr. Wylie-Rosett cautioned that measuring fat against lean without taking other factors into consideration gives slanted data. "It's a confusing subject. If you have any cardiac risk factors, such as a high-cholesterol level, then gaining weight with age puts you at even greater risk. But many people who smoke are thin, and smokers are at greater risk than non-smokers.

"There's also the fact that if you're, say, 65, and develop some form of cancer, and you can't take in food because of your treatment, you have an advantage if you are heavy enough that you have some reserves to fall back on. I don't know the final answer. I suspect some people should be heavy and some light, but I can't say who is who.

"A study done in Hawaii showed that in most age groups, obesity was bad." She smiled. "But look at it this way. If you took a group of people with high blood pressure, the lean people may be harder to treat."

Puzzled, I asked why that was.

"It's simply because you can lower blood pressure by taking off weight, and a lean person with elevated blood pressure has much less weight to take off. That's just a guess of mine, however. But it does make sense."

"Overall," I asked, "would you say a physically active life style offers someone the least risk of heart disease?"

She nodded. "I think so. There are several complicated and complex issues, but an overall prudent life style is definitely associated with a longer and healthier life. Prudence, though, means not going overboard."

"What do you mean?"

"When you eat omega-3 along with omega-6 polyunsaturated vegetable fats, there are some unknowns because omega-6 is not part of the normal metabolic process in humans," Dr. Wylie-Rosett noted.

"What kind of unknowns?"

"We know of no group of people who eat a large quantity of polyunsaturated vegetable fats in a natural situation, in the same way that the Greenland Eskimos, for instance, eat fish. Exactly what happens to polyunsaturated vegetable fats in the body when you also have omega-3 must be more thoroughly explored. I'm certainly not against omega-3. It may not be a miracle cure, but it is certainly intriguing and promising."

"What do we know about what happens to the metabolic process when you have large amounts of omega-3 and omega-6 in your diet?"

Dr. Wylie-Rosett rummaged through a pile of papers on her desk and pulled out an extremely complicated chart. I tried to make sense of it and she smiled, seeing my confusion.

"Basically, when you ingest omega-3, you alter the metabolism of omega-6, a polyunsaturated vegetable oil. There's a delicate balance involved. Consider blood coagulation. If your blood doesn't coagulate well, you have a problem. You can bleed to death from a cut. But if your blood coagulates too efficiently, clots can form in the arteries. That's bad too. You need a proper balance.

"In cardiovascular disease, the balance is skewed toward clotting. A doctor who treats a patient with cardiovascular disease must inhibit blood clotting. Now that's one function we know the omega-3s can perform. But they do other things as well. They appear to have an effect on the inflammatory process in arthritis, and they may affect other diseases. How it all happens is complicated, and from a research standpoint we just don't know enough yet to draw conclusions from it."

As I prepared to leave, I remembered that diabetes and hypertension (high blood pressure) were Dr. Wylie-Rosett's particular area of study. I asked her if omega-3 had any effect on diabetes.

"There are two studies that have been done on diabetes and omega-3, but diabetics have so many health problems, so many complications, that they are usually excluded from most studies. Still, the two studies on diabetes were promising. Unfortunately, the studies weren't randomized and controlled.

"We'll have to wait and see if anything definite results from that work, but we already know enough about omega-3 to say for sure that it has numerous health benefits, especially for the heart."

⌁ ✦ 4 ✦ ⌁

No More Pain: Arthritis, Asthma and Omega-3

By 1985, most scientists agreed that omega-3 fatty acids worked to prevent heart disease. Many, however, remained curious about the other health benefits omega-3 might have for humans. They knew that much of omega-3's effectiveness in preventing heart disease had to do with its action on blood chemistry, and they wanted to learn more about omega-3's mysterious ability to alter the composition of blood. The studies inspired by this curiosity revealed that omega-3 can have an impact on the blood elements that play a role in inflammatory immune system diseases, such as arthritis, lupus and asthma.

ARTHRITIS AND OMEGA-3

Nancy, in her early 60s, is intelligent, outgoing, and attractive. She is married, and she has always worked. "But getting out of bed in the morning had been a problem for years; my arthritis is that severe." She has found some relief with omega-3.

Nancy has osteoarthritis, and her doctor told her that there was little she could do about it except take aspirin. "I always had pain," Nancy told me. "Pain in my shoulder, in my leg . . . but you learn to live with it. I kept taking aspirin and somehow I managed, but I was depressed by the pain."

Finally, after having some x-rays of her shoulder taken, Nancy was told she had a pinched nerve. She started taking anti-inflammatory medication, but four weeks of treatment brought no relief. Finally, the side effects of the medication and a deep depression made her stop.

A friend told her about another woman who had gotten relief with fish oil, and Nancy sent away for some. She took three pills a day—a total of six grams—for a month.

Within the first week, her depression lifted as the pain began to abate. "I was surprised to find that I could get up in the morning, literally jump out of bed and get into the shower. I no longer had to ease myself out of bed as I used to because my shoulder, arm and legs would hurt so. It was always a problem in the morning, at least until after my first cup of coffee, and at night too—but now that's gone." Nancy was totally pain-free after only a month on the fish oil.

Nancy's story is anecdotal evidence of the efficacy of omega-3. As many rheumatologists have pointed out to me, arthritis is a strange disease. People who suffer from it sometimes experience periods of remission during which they are pain-free. But Nancy's experience can give arthritis sufferers hope that omega-3 might offer relief. The work of researchers also holds out that hope.

In order to gain some deeper insights into the action of omega-3, a group of ten scientists decided to perform detailed chemical analyses of the blood of people who had taken fish oil pills. Though they had set out to learn more about omega-3 and heart disease, what they discovered proved of tremendous significance to people suffering from arthritis and other inflammatory diseases.

The scientists, led by Dr. Tak H. Lee, came from a number of different hospitals and medical schools: the Department of Medicine at Harvard Medical School, the Department of Rheumatology and Immunology at Brigham and Woman's Hospital, the Arthritis Unit at Massachusetts General Hospital, and the Department of Chemistry at Harvard University.

Dr. Lee and his associates selected seven healthy male volunteers for the study. The scientists studied males because heart disease is more common among men. (Hormones provide women some protection against heart disease, so its incidence among them is much lower.)

The volunteers ranged in age from 22 to 53 years. Before they were placed on a special diet, blood was drawn from each volunteer for testing. Each participant then took 18 capsules a day of a specially prepared mix of fish oils rich in the omega-3 fatty acids EPA (eicosapentaenoic acid) and DHA (docosahexaenoic acid). The capsules supplied the men with a total of 5.4 grams of omega-3 — the equivalent of eating half a pound of salmon or mackerel — a day. In addition, the pills added a total of 162 calories to each man's daily diet. As a result, some volunteers gained as much as three or four pounds during the six-week study.

The researchers drew blood three weeks into the study, and again after the six-week pill-taking period ended. The blood tests, while revealing nothing new about heart disease, showed suppressed levels of a substance known as leukotriene B4, which is released by the breakdown of platelets in the blood. It can inflame the joints, aggravating inflammatory immune system diseases such as rheumatism and arthritis. Dr. Lee and his associates found that, while there was no difference between the levels of leukotriene B4 found in the blood drawn before the diet and in blood drawn at three weeks, the leukotriene B4 had been "significantly suppressed" in blood drawn six weeks after the start of the omega-3 diet.

I asked a prominent rheumatologist just what the suppression of leukotriene B4 could mean. He has been in practice for many years, and has had very good success controlling his patients' arthritis with drugs, but, "to tell you the truth," he confessed, "I don't really know! I realize that leukotrienes are linked to the functioning of neutrophils (white blood cells) and affect the immune response, but just how, and just how they affect arthritis, I can't tell you. That's rather exotic chemistry and pretty incomprehensible to me. I'm concerned with clinical results, with how my patients respond to treatment. What these researchers are doing is all in a test tube."

Although Dr. Lee's study could not prove to my rheumatologist friend that omega-3 can control the pain suffered by his patients, it does show that fish oils containing omega-3 can suppress leukotrienes. The researchers noted the need for further research because their study involved people who did not have arthritis. They concluded that "... diets enriched with fish-oil-derived fatty acid may have anti-inflammatory effects. ... " In other words, omega-3 may help relieve the pain of arthritis.

The next step was to test omega-3 in people who *did* have arthritis. Scientists needed to conduct controlled studies of large numbers of people. These studies would have to take into account the differences in the experiences of people suffering from arthritis, since the disease progresses at different rates, with different symptoms, in different people.

Dr. Lee's study, along with two others, was published in the prestigious *New England Journal of Medicine*. Their findings electrified the medical world. What doctors had considered a health food fad now appeared to have real significance as a dietary element that could help relieve immune system diseases.

Two new studies, one at the Harvard School of Medicine, and one at Albany Medical College, promptly were commenced to explore the clinical effects of omega-3 on arthritis. The results of these studies were reported to a meeting of the American Rheumatism Association a year later.

Dr. Richard I. Sperling, Associate Professor of Medicine at the Harvard School of Medicine, studied 12 arthritis patients with painful joints. He gave five of them 20 fish oil capsules a day and he gave the other seven placebos (pills with no active ingredients).

Studies in which some participants receive an active drug while others receive a placebo are termed "blind" studies. Blind studies balance the effects taking a pill can have on a patient: even pills containing no active ingredients can sometimes relieve symptoms because of the patient's desire to get well. In a double blind study, neither the doctor nor the patients know until the study is complete, which patients received the placebo and which the active drug. This eliminates any bias the doctor might have regarding the drug's effectiveness.

The participants in Dr. Sperling's study took the pills for ten weeks. During the first six weeks, all of the patients also received an anti-inflammatory drug. After six weeks, the patients taking omega-3 in addition to the anti-inflammatory drug felt much better. The pain in their joints had decreased. But the patients who received the placebo along with the anti-inflammatory drug showed no relief from their arthritic pain.

When Dr. Sperling took the patients off the anti-inflammatory drug, their pain flared up. But for those taking the omega-3, the pain was no worse than it had been before they participated in the experiment. Usually, when arthritis patients stop taking anti-inflammatory drugs, they experience more pain than they did before taking the drugs.

Dr. Sperling concluded that "this suggests that the fish oil does have an anti-arthritic effect."

Dr. Joel M. Kremer, an associate professor of medicine at Albany Medical College, carried out another study. He placed 20 patients with rheumatoid arthritis on 15 capsules of fish oil a day. As a control, he put 20 others on a placebo. All 40 maintained their usual diet during the study.

The patients took the capsules for 14 weeks; then they stopped taking the pills for four weeks. This allowed time for the oil to leave the patients' systems. Then Dr. Kremer did a switch. For 14 more weeks, the patients who had been on the placebo were given fish oil, and the patients who had taken the fish oil were given the placebo.

While taking the fish oil, patients reported about half as many tender and painful joints as they reported at the beginning of the study. They also reported a lessening of fatigue. (Arthritis almost always causes a great deal of fatigue, partly because of the pain it causes, and also because of the tension arthritics feel when they move about.) The researchers noted, however, that the benefits of the fish oil were not permanent. But omega-3 did seem to lessen patients' pain, and without causing any significant side effects. They recommended that studies longer than 14 weeks be conducted.

Dr. Alfred D. Sternberg, chief of cellular immunology at the National Institute of Arthritis and Musculoskeletal and Skin Diseases, feels that the Harvard and Albany studies produced "terrific" results. Still, he warns that proving the clinical effectiveness of omega-3 isn't enough. While fish oil may be valuable, he hopes researchers continue to look for "a drug that will induce remissions."

LUPUS AND OMEGA-3

Another researcher studied omega-3's effects on mice with systemic lupus erythematosus, a form of arthritis. This study found that in mice fish oil produces "the most striking protective effect seen thus far in any animal model of inflammatory disease."

The National Institute of Health, impressed by the results of this study, has begun a large clinical trial to discover the effect of omega-3 on 60 lupus patients. The results are not yet in.

OMEGA-3 AND ASTHMA

Still another group of researchers at the University of California in San Francisco used omega-3 to treat six patients suffering from chronic asthma. Though their immune systems responded to the treatment, their symptoms did not abate. Still, Dr. Donald G. Payan, an assistant professor of medicine at the university, feels that omega-3 may benefit some asthma patients. "It may not have a dramatic effect, but it might allow reduced treatment with other drugs—which would be a significant improvement." He points out, however, the need for further study.

All these studies show that omega-3's value to the human body goes beyond the heart. Omega-3 works on white blood cells and platelets, the factors in the blood related to the immune system. Arthritis and asthma, inflammatory immune system diseases, may be treated with omega-3.

↭ 5 ↭

Holding Out Hope:
Diabetes,
Skin Disorders
and Allergies

----

*I*t was Dr. Wylie-Rosett at the Albert Einstein College of Medicine who had suggested that studies of the effects of omega-3 on diabetes were promising. Diabetes, of course, is a glandular problem: part of the pancreas, in which the hormone insulin is produced, is abnormal and does not produce sufficient insulin. Without the right amount of insulin, the body cannot burn up carbohydrates properly. As a result, there is too much sugar in the diabetic's blood, which can lead to very serious, even deadly, results.

A little research turned up two studies, the more important of which was conducted by Dr. Margaret Albrink and her associates at the University of West Virginia in Morgantown. They had given omega-3 in a fish oil preparation to eight diabetics. Dr. Albrink had reported the results of the study at the Scientific Sessions of the American Diabetes Association in 1986.

When I spoke with Dr. Albrink, she explained that the study had been conducted on eight diabetics who were all type II. "Type II diabetes used to be known as adult diabetes," she said. "It's what we now call non-insulin dependent. People who have it do not need insulin to keep their blood normal and prevent them from going into ketoacidosis." (Ketoacidosis is a dangerous condition in which ketones and acetones accumulate in the blood.) "Type II is not as serious as type I, which used to be called juvenile diabetes. In type I, the patient needs insulin on a daily basis in order to live. In type II, they need it occasionally to keep their blood sugar normal.

"We know that the patients suffering from type II diabetes also have high levels of fats in their blood, cholesterol and triglycerides, and they experience premature hardening of the arteries and increased clumping of their platelets—and, of course, a high incidence of heart attacks. Since we know that omega-3 helps people at risk of coronary artery disease, we wondered if it could also help diabetics."

Were there any effects?

"Not directly," she said, "and we didn't expect it to have any—what we were interested in was what omega-3 might do for the *complications* caused by type II diabetes, because that's what type II diabetics die of—the complications, not the disease."

Dr. Albrink and her associates gave fish oil supplements to eight extremely overweight people with type II diabetes. There were six women and two men, and their mean age was 56. (The disease tends to affect people who are overweight and also more women than men.) The fish oil Dr. Albrink and her associates used was high in that type of omega-3 fatty acid known as eicosapentaenoic acid, EPA. During the time of the study the eight patients kept to their usual diabetic diets.

After one month, Dr. Albrink found very definite changes in the blood of all eight patients. The triglycerides in their blood decreased by almost a third and cholesterol levels went down from an average of 270 to 248. The HDL increased and the LDL decreased, and the ability of platelets to form clumps, one cause of clotting, also went down—all positive changes in terms of coronary artery disease. The patients' weight, blood sugar and blood pressure did not change.

Dr. Albrink told me that the fish oil tasted so unpleasant that although they started the study with ten patients, two volunteers dropped out after the first month, leaving only eight to complete it. This, she noted, was probably because the daily fish oil was given by spoon rather than by capsule. In any event, she concludes that omega-3 "has a beneficial effect on type II diabetes by decreasing triglycerides, increasing HDL and cutting down on platelet aggregation." By doing all this it also cuts down on the other serious health problems that can face diabetics, problems that may lead to death. She believes that the results are encouraging enough to warrant a close look at omega-3 fatty acids as another tool to help people with type II diabetes who also have heart and blood vessel disorders. Intending to go ahead with larger studies, Dr. Albrink confides that in the future she'll use capsules instead of spoonfuls!

The second study that Dr. Wylie-Rosett had mentioned was done by a team of seven researchers from Great Britain, some from Queen Elizabeth College at the University of London and others from Norwich Park Hospital. These researchers gave fish oil containing omega-3 to a group of type I (juvenile) diabetics. Their rationale was based on the fact that platelets in the blood of diabetics clump more easily, have shorter life spans and break down more quickly than platelets in the blood of well people. In breaking down, these platelets release a type of thromboxane which can be harmful to the body and cause albumin to appear in the urine.

Albumin excreted in the urine is common among diabetics: it indicates a breakdown in the protein of the body. Any substance that inhibits the production of thromboxane should also reduce the amount of albumin in the urine. And cutting down on the amount excreted is helpful.

Another reason omega-3 may be helpful for diabetics is that any abnormality in the platelets can well be a cause of the breaks and clots in small blood vessels that cause diabetics so much trouble. These problems can lead to very large ones—blindness and the possible need for amputation are ever-present threats in type I diabetes.

In this British study, type I diabetics were selected at random to receive either fish oil capsules rich in omega-3 or placebos of olive oil. The patients were all between the ages of 30 and 59. They were asked not to take any aspirin for two weeks before the study started and for as long as it lasted. (Aspirin can keep the blood from clotting, and the researchers feared it might interfere with the results.)

The patients were examined at the start of the study, after three weeks and after six weeks. Nineteen were given the fish oil capsules, and 22 were given the olive oil placebos.

The results of this very carefully controlled study were in part puzzling. In general, there seemed no doubt that the production of thromboxane was lowered by the omega-3, more so after six weeks of treatment than after only three. This is of some benefit to diabetics, but curiously, there was no evidence in this study of a lessening of the platelets' ability to clump. By contrast, in similar studies with non-diabetics, platelet clumping was lessened. Obviously, the researchers speculated, there was something in the disease itself, in diabetes, that prevented this beneficial response. Another unexpected finding was that no changes in urinary albumin excretion were found in any of the patients.

Further, the fish oil supplements *increased* the diabetics' cholesterol, an increase that could lead to an increased risk of coronary artery disease. However, this increase in cholesterol was not found in other studies of people taking omega-3. It may be the disease itself that causes the rise, or, the researchers suggest, more likely the rise in cholesterol might be due to the 30 percent of saturated fat—an unusually high amount—in the fish oil capsules they chose for the study! This might also have accounted for the lack of change in urinary excretion.

They concluded that diabetics may be unusually sensitive to changes in fat intake, especially since the fish oil was given in *addition* to their regular diet. Although they observed some potentially good effects in diabetics given omega-3, they warn against the possible adverse effects of a fish oil capsule supplement in type I diabetes.

It would seem logical, then, that the next step in research would be to include at least three omega-3-rich fish *meals* in diabetic diets instead of giving them fish oil capsules containing extra fat.

GOOD NEWS FOR THE SKIN

In my search for other conditions that have been helped by omega-3 fatty acids, I discovered that there have been some interesting studies by dermatologists that seem to indicate a possible role for omega-3 fatty acids in treating eczema and psoriasis. Both of these conditions have been linked to the breakdown of prostaglandin in the body. Prostaglandin is a naturally occurring substance in the body; when it breaks down, it produces substances that act as irritating and inflaming agents.

Dr. Charles N. Ellis of the Department of Dermatology at the University of Michigan has found that when patients with these troubling skin conditions are given fish oil capsules, the cell membranes in their skin are enriched with eicosapentaenoic acid (EPA), and fewer breakdown products of prostaglandin are released. Eczema and psoriasis were both helped by omega-3.

Help for people suffering from skin allergies has been reported from Great Britain. Dr. T.H. Lee of the Department of Medicine at Guy's Hospital in London found that a diet rich in fish oil has the ability to change the "inflammatory components of the allergy response." In other words, the EPA in omega-3 inhibits the production of irritating material just as it did in Dr. Ellis' study. But the patients Dr. Lee worked with were allergy sufferers; the omega-3 diet he fed them "modulated human allergies . . . at the clinical, cellular and biochemical levels."

Dr. Lee was able to conclude that there were actual *physical* changes. The importance of this lies in the fact that so many "good" results in allergy problems in the past have been due, not to a physical change, but to a psychological one. Dr. Lee's work produced an improvement not in the head, but in the skin!

6

Omega-3 and Migraine Headaches

D r. Robert Hitzemann is an associate professor in the Department of Psychiatry of the School of Medicine at the State University of New York in Stonybrook. In 1981, four years before the publication of the three articles in the *New England Journal of Medicine* that reported the effects of omega-3 on the cardiovascular system, Dr. Hitzemann had begun his examination of the cellular effects that might lead to migraine headaches.

"I was interested in the biology of migraine," he explained when I talked with him. "The popular idea then was that it might be a blood disease, that the platelets in a migraine sufferer were abnormal, and there was a disturbance in the secretion of serotonin." Serotonin is a breakdown product of blood platelets, and it can cause blood vessels to constrict. It can also affect the function of nerves. And since omega-3 can help blood platelets from clumping and breaking down to release serotonin, it made sense to try to link it to migraine headaches, which are caused by the action of nerves and blood vessels.

Dr. Hitzemann's study found that the platelets in migraine sufferers were deficient in omega-3 fatty acids. People who were what he called "infrequent migraine sufferers" had significantly more omega-3 in their platelets than people who were frequent sufferers.

"What we hoped to do," he explained, "was to change the frequent sufferers to infrequent ones. Never mind a cure. Just lessening the number of attacks would be a great boon to migraine sufferers.

"Migraine headaches are a devastating problem, one that affects women five times more frequently than it does men. Twenty-five percent of all women of child-bearing years have migraine headaches."

Does this have anything to do with female hormones?

"I think so. Migraine tends to occur around the menstrual period. Actually we know very little about the biology of migraine. We do know that there's a genetic tendency to it, that it runs in families."

To test his theory that increasing the amount of omega-3 in the diet would help migraine sufferers, Dr. Hitzemann selected 15 frequent sufferers. "There were seven men and eight women—an unusual mix when you consider its occurrence in the general population."

Dr. Hitzemann used one-gram capsules of fish oil, each containing 350 mg of a mix of eicosapentaenoic acid (EPA) and docosahexaenoic acid (DHA), both omega-3 fatty acids. "We gave each patient a fixed dose, five grams at each meal, 15 grams a day no matter what their weight or sex was. The capsules added some extra calories to their diet, ten calories per capsule, but to overcome that we kept them on an isocaloric diet, that is a diet on which they'd neither gain nor lose weight."

I asked about the diet, and he explained that it was the American Heart Diet of 300 mg of cholesterol a day. "It's a moderately low-cholesterol diet, the kind you give to people who are possible candidates for a heart attack. The patients all had access to dieticians who could show them how to prepare foods.

"We asked them to keep a daily diary of their headaches and the foods they ate and the stresses they were under. What we were looking for was any event that might precipitate a migraine attack."

What type of study was it?

"A double-blind one with placebos. Neither the people who gave the capsules nor the patients who took them knew which contained omega-3 and which were placebos. The placebo we used was a vegetable oil that looked like the fish oil. We put all 15, those receiving the fish oil and those receiving the placebo, on a six-week course of treatment. Then we took them off the capsules for three weeks. This was to allow the omega-3 to wash out of their systems.

"After the wash-out, we did a cross-over. The ones who had omega-3 were given the placebo, and those who had been taking the placebos were given omega-3. This went on for another six weeks.

"You must understand that all 15 of these patients had frequent migraines—at least two attacks a week. These were classic cases, people who had migraines with neurological symptoms, visual symptoms, the inability to speak—this is a fairly rare group."

Why was he so insistent on classic cases?

"Because there's an argument that migraine is related to muscle tension, and I wanted to weed out any such cases. All of our patients had tried conventional medication—beta blockers, ergot derivatives, antidepressants—and had failed to get any relief from them.

"Analyzing our results, we found that five out of seven men and three out of eight women got better. We saw that as very significant."

What did he mean by "better"?

"Their responses varied. We considered a 30 percent reduction in symptoms high, and a 70 percent reduction the maximum.

"While we concluded that in some patients omega-3 had been beneficial, this was only the beginning. We have to move ahead. I'm going to continue the study with a new group of 100 patients, and I'll increase the dosage of fish oil, use a significantly larger amount of omega-3, particularly for women."

What about a fish diet rather than the capsules? Could they get enough omega-3 that way?

"They'd have to eat a lot of fish—a lot! Three capsules a day—well, it's more like a drug than a food additive. They have to take enough to affect their body chemistry. You need a lot to do that. My advice is, if you have migraine headaches, see a doctor first. There is a lot of good therapy available for it. There is a lot you can do without using capsules. It's only when you don't respond to any conventional therapy that you should consider omega-3."

Repeating the fact that he made his patients adhere to the low-cholesterol American Heart Diet, Dr. Hitzemann stressed that, "it may well be that the two components, a diet with cold-water fish containing omega-3 plus the fish oil, are responsible for the good results in eight out of 15 patients. If you suffer from migraines, you cannot eat as usual and take fish oil. You must also cut down on cholesterol and saturated fats."

Why?

"It's quite simple. Cholesterol and saturated fats will compete with omega-3 for sites in the body where they will be effective. You have to think of these fatty acids as drugs. Omega-3 has one effect; cholesterol and saturated fats have another. All compete for the same sites. Give omega-3 a chance to get there first by cutting the odds, by allowing less cholesterol and fewer saturated fats into the race. Omega-3 will then have a chance to get into the platelets."

In a 1984 issue of *Lancet*, the British medical journal, I came across a report from the National Hospital for Nervous Diseases in London that noted that in some patients, food allergies had caused migraines. Migraine sufferers with food allergies have blood platelets that tend to clump together more readily than normal. An agent that reduces the clumping, such as omega-3, should have beneficial effects.

Migraine sufferers have traditionally used ergot derivatives that work on the inflamed blood vessels in the head. Omega-3 may well prove to be a significant element in the physician's bag of promising cures.

7

Breast Feeding And Breast Cancer

*A*nimal research has yielded some findings that may prove of particular interest to women. The importance of omega-3 fatty acids for pregnant and breast-feeding women and for women concerned about breast cancer has to do with the different ways the body makes use of the fats it receives through diet. Omega-3 plays the role of a "good fat" in the development of fetuses and infants; it also inhibits the action of "bad fat" in the development of cancer cells.

INFANT DEVELOPMENT AND OMEGA-3

Dr. William E. Connor and his associates at Oregon Health Sciences University in Portland used rhesus monkeys, close relatives of humans, in their research of the effects of omega-3 on fetal development. They fed pregnant females a diet deficient in omega-3, both during pregnancy and after they gave birth. The babies born to these monkeys developed poor eyesight and other eye ailments. The eyesight of four of the baby monkeys later improved tremendously when the researchers switched them to a diet rich in omega-3.

DHA (docosahexaenoic acid), an omega-3 fatty acid, represents one of the primary components of eye and brain tissue and may be the brain food Grandma told you about! The findings of the Oregon researchers reflected the particular importance of DHA to the healthy growth of these tissues in embryos and infants in their first year of life. This study added to scientists' understanding of the brain by showing how the addition of omega-3 to the diet could measurably change the development of the nervous system.

The brain, Dr. Connor concluded, has "a remarkable capacity to change its fatty acid content after a fish-oil diet. There is a greater liability of the fatty acids of the brain than previously thought."

Dr. Connor and his associates next went on to investigate whether consumption of omega-3 fatty acids changed the composition of human milk. Human milk contains small but significant amounts of DHA, manufactured in the liver from linolenic acid, another omega-3. The linoleic acid so common in western diets is an omega-6 fatty acid. Because of its similarity to omega-3, the presence of linoleic acid in the body inhibits production of DHA, thus depriving fetuses and nursing infants of a vital nutrient. Infant formulas based on soybean oil contain a great deal of DHA, but babies absorb the DHA in human milk much more easily.

Fish oil provides a good supplementary source of DHA when the liver cannot produce enough, so the Oregon team set out to discover whether a mother's omega-3-rich diet could boost the amount of DHA in the milk available to a nursing baby.

In the study, six nursing women took five grams of fish oil daily for four weeks. This is the equivalent of about three ounces of a high-fat fish a day. A four week "washout" period followed, during which the women took no fish oil in order to allow the omega-3 to pass out of their systems. After the "washout" period, five of the women took 10 grams a day for two weeks. The women reported no problems in taking the capsules other than a "slight fish taste," and no change in the nursing behavior of their babies.

The researchers found that the omega-3 content of the mothers' milk increased very soon after they started taking the fish oil, and that it remained high during the first week after they stopped. They pointed out that "this, of course, would increase the infant's intake of this important fatty acid, and could conceivably influence development and growth." Though the Oregon study did not prove that a mother's intake of omega-3 would definitely influence the neurological development of her nursing baby, the possibility remains that fish *is*, in fact, brain food. If so, pregnant and nursing women might contribute to the development of their babies by adding cold-water fish to their diets.

BREAST CANCER AND OMEGA-3

Another area where animal experimentation has yielded some surprising results is in cancer research. Drs. Rashida A. Karmali, Jane Marsh and Charles Fuchs, three researchers from the Sloan-Kettering Institute in New York, conducted an experiment using rats. Their results suggest that omega-3 may be a valuable tool in the fight against breast cancer.

The populations of North America and northwest Europe experience a high incidence of breast cancer, which appears to be linked to a diet rich in fats. Yet Greenland Eskimos, who take in large amounts of fat, have a low rate of death from breast cancer. The Sloan-Kettering team decided that "the link between fat intake and breast cancer must therefore be evaluated with care."

The researchers implanted breast tumors in female laboratory rats. They fed the rats a diet rich in fish oil for a week before they implanted the cancerous tumors and then for three weeks after. A control group of rats with implanted tumors received a diet without fish oil. Autopsies later showed that those fed the fish oil had developed much smaller tumors that the control group: omega-3 had inhibited the growth of breast cancer in rats.

Scientists have known for some time that a diet rich in ordinary (i.e. omega-6) fat increases the risk of breast cancer. But when the researchers examined the tumors of the sacrificed rats, they found that omega-3 fatty acids had replaced omega-6 fatty acids in tissue fats, blood and platelets. And the tumors had hardly grown.

Another study seems to support the findings of the Sloan-Kettering group. A team of scientists at The Stuart Pharmaceutical Company found a reduction in the number of cancerous tumors among rats whose normal diets had been supplemented with seaweed. Brown kelp seaweed contains a good deal of omega-3, and is a part of the traditional diet in Japan, a country with a low incidence of breast cancer.

More research on this subject is clearly warranted. A close examination of the diets of women who have developed breast cancer and of those who have survived the disease might provide more information on the connection between omega-3 and breast cancer risk reduction. A study in which women with breast cancer are placed on omega-3 supplements may provide even more clues. And scientists may find further leads as to why populations that eat a great deal of fish have low rates of breast cancer. Fish and seaweed, though the combination may not seem a gourmet's delight, may offer protection against breast cancer; and, as my sushi-loving son pointed out to me, a slice of tuna wrapped in seaweed can also be a real culinary treat!

⇜ *Part II* ⇝

THE OMEGA-3 DIET PLANS

8

Diet, Nutrition And Fish Oil

Recent reports of studies on the importance of fats and cholesterol have increased public consciousness of the role that diet plays in good health. Like most health-conscious consumers, I sometimes feel a little overwhelmed by conflicting advice on what's bad, what's good, what's in, and what's out *this* year. So I decided to continue my personal investigation into healthy eating by discussing the matter with Dr. Alexander, my cardiologist. If I trusted him to care for me in a life-threatening health crisis, I could certainly rely on him to tell me what constituted a good diet.

"The average American," he told me, "eats about 40 grams of fat a day: almost an ounce and a half, which is too much. Someone who has no sign of heart disease, but would like to guard against it, should start by lowering the amount of saturated fat they consume, especially animal fat. There's really no question but that consuming animal fat over the years can lead to hardening of the coronary arteries in the heart, the carotid artery in the head, the renal arteries in the kidneys, and the arteries in the legs. Those arteries get plugged up with cholesterol plaque. Taking in all that fat can also predispose a person to certain forms of cancer—colon cancer, in particular. And then there's the matter or reducing cholesterol intake.

"Let me make a distinction between saturated fats and cholesterol," he continued. "Cholesterol is a kind of fat, but it has a different structure. It's found in meats, red meat in particular, which also contain saturated fats. In fact, when you lower your cholesterol intake, you usually lower the amount of fat you take in."

I asked Dr. Alexander how he would assess the relative dangers of saturated fats and cholesterol."

"They're equally dangerous," he said without hesitation. "Consumers should carefully read food labels when they shop. A lot of products list partially hydrogenated oils, which are saturated fats, in their contents. Palm oil and coconut oil are also saturated fats, even though they contain no cholesterol."

He stressed that people should use oil in their cooking; they just had to be careful about which oil they chose. The rule of thumb is that the harder the fat, the more potential danger it poses. In other words, go light on butter, use regular margarine more frequently, and liquid margarine yet more often.

"Is there still any question about a connection between eating saturated fats and cholesterol and developing heart disease?" I asked.

"In my mind, no. We know that people with an elevated cholesterol level in their blood have a much higher incidence of coronary heart disease. That's clear-cut. And we know that you can lower your cholesterol level through diet as well as by taking medicine. The only question has been: will lowering your cholesterol lessen your chances of getting heart disease?

"Two years ago, however, studies in the United States showed conclusively that you reduce the risk of coronary artery disease by lowering your cholesterol level. I have no doubt that people on a low-fat, low-cholesterol diet have less chance of developing heart disease, or, if they already have the disease, have a decreased risk of experiencing the chest pains of angina or a heart attack."

ON TO OTHER FATS

"We're clear on saturated fats," I said. "But what about monounsaturated and polyunsaturated fats?" I told him that I knew they were less harmful than the saturated variety, but could they actually help to lower serum cholesterol?

In the case of polyunsaturated fats, his answer was yes.

"Polyunsaturated fats lower cholesterol by affecting its metabolism in the liver. In the intestine, these fats prevent LDL, the substance that facilitates the deposition of cholesterol on your artery walls, from getting into the bloodstream. And they help HDL, which helps remove those deposits from artery walls, to circulate.

"As for monounsaturated fat, it's neither bad nor good. It may have a mild lowering effect, but it is not as significant as the polyunsaturated fatty acids."

"Which kinds of polyunsaturated fats should we include in our diets?"

"Safflower oil, soybean oil, corn oil."

Then I asked him for some general tips for healthy eating that everyone should follow.

He said that he tells all his patients to eliminate egg yolks from their diets, since this substance is extremely high in cholesterol. The egg whites, however, present no problem. After that, he added, "minimize or eliminate red meat, and eat more fish and chicken. Prepare chicken without the skin, or at least remove the skin before you eat the meat. It's the skin that has the cholesterol, and it leaches down into the meat. Sure, it makes it tender—but at a price."

This brought us to animal fats. I knew that he would veto any organ meat—liver, kidneys, brains—because of their high cholesterol content. But what about veal?

That produced a shrug. "Veal is controversial. We used to think it was good for you because it wasn't a red meat, but it does have a fairly high cholesterol content. I think it's better than red meat, but not as good as chicken or fish."

"Pork?" I asked hopefully.

He shuddered at that. "Awful, really, in terms of fat."

I confessed to feeling envious of the average person who could at least have a meat meal once a week and still keep their blood vessels in good shape. A person like myself, with a cholesterol level above 200, couldn't even take a chance on eating lamb. Was there anything else for me besides fish and chicken?

Jon touted vegetarian meals. Beans or tofu could supply the protein. And he advised me to stay with fresh fruits and vegetables, simply because they tasted better.

Thinking of the Chinese wok for stir frying, which uses very little oil, I then asked him what happens to a polyunsaturated fat when it's heated for cooking.

"When omega-3 fish oils are heated for cooking they don't change."

"And how about cooking with olive oil, a monounsaturated fat?"

"It's very good."

"Thank heavens!" I allowed myself to think gratefully of pasta with oil and garlic, salads with oil and vinegar . . . and remembered that in the part of Italy where olive oil is used for cooking, the incidence of heart disease is low. Dr. Alexander confirmed this, and pointed out that the Mediterranean diet also included fish.

"What about dairy products?" I asked next.

"Try to eliminate them," he responded. "Use skim milk. There's a no-fat yogurt on the market and all kinds of cholesterol-free products. For the average, healthy person, I'd say simply be careful."

"Ice cream?"

"Forget it!"

"Sorbet? Tofutti?"

"Tofutti is loaded with calories; sorbet can contain a lot of sugar."

At this point he reflected for a moment, and then added: "The patients who give me the most trouble about eating are the ones in their 40s and 50s. The typical middle-aged person at risk is someone whose taste buds are used to too much salt, preservatives, fatty foods—fat, after all, carries the aroma of food, and smell plays an important part in taste. It's hard to change."

Since he had raised the subject of taste, what about salt? I knew it was bad for people with high blood pressure, but what about the rest of us?

"Cook without salt," he replied firmly. "If necessary, add it at the table." He was especially concerned with the amount of salt we eat in processed foods—canned soups and vegetables, frozen foods with sauces. "You'll see salt or monosodium glutamate, another source of sodium, on every label. Read labels, and remember it's the sodium in salt that does the dirty work."

I told Jon that I was reminded of the old story of the king who had a royal fit over the matter of taste. "The king had an argument with his cook over what was the sweetest thing in the world. He said sugar and the cook said salt! Furious at having his word contradicted, the king ordered the dissenter beheaded. The cook begged the king to let him prove his point, and his highness relented, giving him a week. During that time the cook served absolutely no salt to the king. Sure enough, after seven days, with tears in his eyes, the king admitted that salt was the sweetest thing in the world."

Jon laughed, and then he wondered what had happened to the king's blood pressure that week. "Salt causes the blood to retain water," he told me, "and that increases the amount of blood in the body, which in turn raises the blood pressure. Salt also firms up the artery walls, increasing their resistance to liquid pressure. This forces the heart to pump harder to get the blood through, also elevating blood pressure."

The doctor was also down on sugar. "Processed or refined sugar is harmful, not only for diabetics but for heart patients too. If you must have sugar in your diet, take it in the form of natural sweets—fruit."

I asked about brown sugar.

"It's still sugar, still processed. All the so-called natural sugars in health food stores are processed sugars. They're bad for you."

Was there such a thing as unprocessed sugar?

"No. Honey is the nearest thing to it, but it's still sugar, although probably not as harmful as white sugar. Any kind of sugar should be limited to occasional desserts and coffee. Sugar substitutes are better than the real thing, but then we get into the question of carcinogens in these substances. We still don't know the whole story on that subject, although I'd say aspartame (NutraSweet™) is probably the least harmful."

ALCOHOL

"And drinking—what about alcohol and coronary health?"

He saw no problem in moderate drinking, "say two glasses of wine a day." But he surprised me when he suggested that alcohol may yet turn out to be a very healthy food substance.

"How?"

"It might lower cholesterol. We know that it can raise the amount of HDL in the body and lower LDL. There was something in a National Institutes of Health report about a year ago, and some recent stuff about beer in modest amounts."

He handed me a newspaper clipping, and explained that this study involving 17,000 Canadians "found that beer drinkers were substantially healthier than non-beer drinkers. Now that's moderate beer drinking. Those who drank it one or more times a day had less sickness than expected. On the other hand, heavy drinkers, those who drank 35 or more pints a week, were sick more often than usual. Of course, that doesn't necessarily mean that the beer drinkers who didn't get sick owe their health to the brew. They may just lead healthier lives, or may not like to admit illness. But I suspect it's the beer, the barley in it."

"And just one or two glasses a day?"

"That's right, or white wine. That should help the arteries. Of course, there are the extra calories, but you could drink one of the low-calorie wines."

"What about hard liquor?"

"Now wine and hard liquor haven't the advantage of barley, but a prudent amount of liquor is good—but remember, modest amounts."

"And what about exercise in all of this? Does it help get cholesterol down and HDL up?"

"It can have a beneficial effect on cholesterol and raise HDL levels, but we don't know why. A recent study in California, on a large group of people over many years, did show a prolongation of life. But even if it doesn't *do* anything, it's clear that people who exercise regularly are less dependent on medicine and feel better about themselves."

IT TAKES A FAT TO LOWER A FAT

We'd finally arrived at the crux of the matter: what did the doctor think of the fish oil capsules that contain omega-3? How effective are they? Over lunch in the hospital cafeteria, Dr. Alexander began with the epidemiological data.

"It's very convincing. The Greenland Eskimos clearly have a much lower incidence of heart disease. Yet what they eat—whale and seal blubber and cold-water fish—is loaded with fat. We've only recently taken a look at the fat content of blubber. Fat in marine life clearly differs from that in vegetables and land animals simply because it's higher in omega-3 fatty acids.

"Now that we know that," he continued, "we have to ask how and why that difference affects us, and then ask how we can translate that knowledge into a better diet."

"What do we know about the way omega-3 in our diet helps us?" I asked.

"Fish oil affects the functioning of our blood platelets," he told me. "Platelets are responsible for the stickiness of the blood. Omega-3 makes them less sticky, or less reactive. It also affects the prostaglandins, decreasing the production of thromboxane-A^2."

"And thromboxane is . . . ?

"A substance that constricts the blood vessels. Another product of the prostaglandin breakdown is prostacyclin, which dilates the blood vessels and inhibits platelets from aggregating, thus decreasing their stickiness."

He smiled at my puzzled look. "You and your readers don't have to know everything about that. Just be aware that taking a lot of omega-3 can result in a low incidence of heart attacks."

"But how?" I continued to press for details.

He went over it again. "It affects the production of vasoactive substances—prostacyclin, thromboxane-A^2—decreasing release of a platelet growth factor. The growth factor would cause cells in artery walls to proliferate, ultimately bringing on atherosclerosis. It also lowers cholesterol a modest amount and lowers triglycerides dramatically; and it increases HDL. How's that for a double-double-barreled effort?"

Backtracking for a moment, I zeroed in on triglycerides. Since he had said that omega-3 lowers triglyceride levels dramatically, I wanted to know what was the significance of an elevated level of this substance, and how they were related to cholesterol.

"I'm not sure," he answered. "There is debate about whether an elevated triglyceride level is a risk factor for coronary artery disease—it's been bandied about a great deal. Many years ago we thought it was. Then we thought maybe not. Now, once again, we believe it may be a risk factor—not as much as cholesterol, but usually the two go together. If one is elevated, the other is likely to be."

"Are triglycerides a part of cholesterol?"

"No, it's a different type of fat circulating in the blood, a separate fat in a different fraction of the lipoproteins."

I could feel myself getting out of my depth. "Lipoproteins?"

"The fat bound to the protein—but let's not get into all that complication. Maybe triglycerides are a risk factor, maybe not. If so, it's not as important as cholesterol, and the omega-3 oils are the most dramatic in lowering the triglyceride fraction of the blood."

So it took a fat to lower a fat—but why?

"The mechanism isn't clear, but it probably affects the liver, which manufactures cholesterol. Alter that mechanism and you lower cholesterol levels.

"So omega-3 has a primary effect on the blood fats, cholesterol and triglycerides, and a secondary effect on the platelets and the production of prostaglandin and its products," he said, summing up the ground we had covered.

"Oh yes," Dr. Alexander added, "it also lowers blood pressure, and affects arthritis, diabetes, prostate and breast cancer, migraine headaches and other conditions connected with the prostaglandin pathway."

"What about fish oil capsules versus a meal of fish?" I asked, as we got to the heart of the matter.

"Almost all of the clinical studies are done with fish oil capsules," he said, "but the epidemiological studies are based on people who eat a diet rich in fish. We have to discover how much fish oil consumption per day is necessary for beneficial effects, and if the capsules have any harmful side effects. Then, too, we want to find out if taking fish oil in a concentrated form, as in capsules, is equal to getting omega-3 naturally in a fish diet."

"How much omega-3 should one consume?" I wondered.

"If you're eating cold-water fish, have at least two fish meals—three-and-a-half ounce servings—a week. Three would be better."

I doubted if many people ate such small portions.

"Maybe not, but that's enough to help. A quarter of a pound or more won't hurt. Here's a good regimen: fish at two evening meals and at one or two lunches, perhaps canned sardines or tuna for lunch."

"Water-packed or oil-packed tuna?"

"Water leaches out the omega-3 from the fish. I'd advise fish packed in its own oil or in olive oil or in a polyunsaturated oil like soybean oil."

"When taking capsules instead of eating fish, how many capsules should one take?"

"There's still a question about dosage. This is a new area and the results are not all in. Some of the studies used tremendous amounts of capsules, 20 a day. I think, with the amount of omega-3 in the average capsule, one or two capsules three times a day would give you enough for cardiac protection. For the other conditions—arthritis, migraine—we'll just have to wait until the results of some more controlled studies come in."

He shook his head. "Americans tend to want a quick fix. They say, 'I don't want to watch my diet. If I can take a pill, okay.' That's the problem with the fish oil. However, if I have a patient with a clear-cut elevated triglyceride level, I give him one or two capsules of fish oil a day and monitor his blood picture."

"Is there any danger from an overdose of omega-3?"

"Well, look at some of the Eskimo data. They consume far more omega-3 than the average American fish lover can take in comfortably, and though they have a low incidence of heart disease and heart attacks, their incidence of stroke is high. That could be related to the fact that these people have blood that doesn't clot well, caused by omega-3 consumption."

"How could that cause a stroke?"

"A hemorrhage could occur because the artery wall is weakened. It usually happens only with age, but when you interfere with the artery walls—and omega-3 does that—you may be lessening the chances of coronary artery disease but putting yourself at risk in the case of stroke. Because of this, I would not suggest that someone take an aspirin a day and the fish oil capsules as well unless they have a definite disease that's being treated, or they are at risk of coronary heart disease."

"As I am?"

"Yes. You can add that daily aspirin to your cold-water fish diet, but why take the capsules? Let's wait until all the data is in."

Responding to my doubtful look, he added, "One or two capsules a day probably wouldn't hurt the average person. Neither would a tablespoonful of cod liver oil. That might be enough protection."

It was time to go. Afterwards, I was still not certain about the issue of fish oil capsules versus a fish oil diet. I felt that I needed to do further research, and learn more about cholesterol, the prostaglandin pathway, and just how omega-3 worked.

9

No Quick Fixes:
Capsules Versus
A Fish Diet

*V*irtually every medical expert I have consulted in preparing this book has stressed the necessity of eating a well-balanced diet. Overeating, eating poorly, smoking, heavy intake of salt and refined sugar, caffeine and saturated fats—all of these will certainly promote heart disease, cancer, high blood pressure, diabetes and a host of other illnesses. The body *is*, after all, a complex machine: fail to give it the best kind of fuels and proper maintenance, and one day the parts will break down. And no one dietary component used as a supplement can be a quick fix against years of neglect or daily sins of omission and excess.

And so it is with omega-3. The wondrous ability of cold-water fish oil to affect blood chemistry and reverse some of the consequences of illness or self-neglect shows extraordinary potential to lower the risks of some of our most killing diseases. But by itself, it cannot perform miracles. Thus I think it necessary to amplify what Dr. Alexander touched on in the last chapter.

The sudden availability of a profusion of omega-3 capsules is bound to be confusing to the average consumer. Any good thing taken in excess can become of questionable value. The potential for indiscriminate use of fish-oil capsules was considered so important that it became a theme at the American Heart Association News Conference in Dallas in November 1986. Dr. Roger Illingworth, in his remarks to the conference, pointed out that there is a big difference between substituting fish for meat in the diet and taking fish-oil capsules. "The studies that have shown a lipid-lowering effect and an anti-thrombotic effect," he noted, "have used mega-doses of fish oil that I think must be regarded as pharmacological." He stressed that these dosages could not be compared to taking two to four capsules of fish oil a day.

His opinions were echoed by Dr. Edwin L. Bierman, professor of medicine at Seattle's University of Washington, who pointed out that "the use of fish or fish-oil capsules in managing disorders of the blood fats is a very different proposition from the use of fish as part of a prudent diet." Meals that substitute fish for meat to prevent possible coronary artery problems are "perfectly well justified," while using fish or the capsules to *treat* diseases is still experimental. He suggested caution be exercised in the use of fish-oil capsules.

CAUTIONS AND CONTENTS

Comparing a diet of fish to the use of capsules is difficult because the various fish oils on the market contain different amounts of omega-3, and in varying proportions to their other components. In some brands, omega-3 accounts for only 30 percent of total fat. Others, claiming to contain 50 percent omega-3, in fact have only 42 percent. Still others have as little as 20 percent. Another important consideration is that almost every fish oil available (Warner Lambert's Promega™ being the exception) has sizeable amounts of cholesterol and saturated fats in addition to their omega-3 content, as illustrated by the following chart, based on a 100-gram edible portion:

Fish Oils	*Omega-3 Content*	*Saturated Fat*	*Cholesterol*
Menhaden Oil	21.7 g	33.6 g	521 mg
Salmon Oil	20.9 g	23.8 g	285 mg
Cod Liver Oil	19.2 g	17.6 g	570 mg
Herring Oil	12.0 g	19.2 g	766 mg
Max EPA™ Capsules	29.4 g	25.4 g	600 mg

Fish Oils	Omega-3 Content	Saturated Fat	Cholesterol
Proto-Chol™ Capsules	30.0 g	20.0 g	600 mg
Promega™ Capsules	50.0 g	10.0 g	0.7 mg

There is reason for further caution. Drs. Malcolm B. Baird and Jane L. Hough of the Masonic Medical Research Laboratory in Utica, New York, analyzed the vitamin A content in four commercially sold fish-oil capsules. They found that if people were to take the recommended dosage of capsules, they would be at risk for vitamin A poisoning. As a result of their research, they strongly recommended that doctors caution patients about the hazards of vitamin A overdosage when prescribing fish-oil supplements; consumers attempting fish-oil supplementation on their own should proceed with caution.

Should the average person with no sign of coronary artery disease take fish-oil capsules as a general dietary supplement? Dr. Illingworth felt there was little evidence to suggest that two or three capsules added to the typical American daily diet was any protection against atherosclerosis. He did, however, recommend giving one capsule daily to someone who was definitely allergic to fish.

Last but not least, questions were raised about side effects and interactions. The panel of scientists pointed to a possible increase in bleeding time—the length of time it takes blood to coagulate—that could be hazardous to someone injured in an accident or undergoing emergency surgery. And for heart disease patients and others who already use aspirin as an anti-coagulant, the combination of substances might also dangerously prolong bleeding time.

The general feeling of the doctors at the Dallas conference was that, while the results of omega-3 studies are exciting, there may be dangers in taking large amounts of the capsules or large amounts of the omega-3-rich oils offered commercially. The best course for the average person is to change his or her diet to include cold-water fish two or three times a week and to round out that diet with low-cholesterol foods and foods low in saturated fats. They all stressed that it is misleading to tell the general public that it can benefit by taking fish oil pills while continuing to eat high-fat, high-cholesterol foods.

AND NOW A WORD FROM
CORPORATE AMERICA

When any panacea is uncovered, corporate America leaps in. For example, after the health benefits of dietary fiber and calcium were publicized, the market was flooded with fiber and calcium products. Companies that manufacture vitamins and other food supplements are already giving the same hyped-up treatment to fish oil capsules.

The capsules have been available from relatively small companies for years, but now large pharmaceutical houses like Warner Lambert and Squibb are producing them too.

One doctor involved in omega-3 research seemed concerned that the hype promoted by these companies would cause people to replace good diets with the quick fix of pill popping. Dr. W. Virgil Brown, Professor of Medicine at Mount Sinai School of Medicine in New York has cautioned that "we just don't know enough to promote wide use of these pills."

On the other side of the fence, drug companies argue with some logic that some people just cannot be kept to a sensible diet. Lawrence Haverkart, new products director for Warner Lambert, feels that doctors want something like the fish-oil capsules to recommend to people who "just cannot give up eggs."

The doctors I talked to were generally dubious of the claims made about the capsules. "I have patients coming in every day with a bottle of fish-oil capsules asking me how many they should take," a New York cardiologist told me. "I'm not at all sure of what to advise them, but I do suggest adding cold-water fish to their diet. Based on what I've read, I think that eating fish two or three times a week is just as beneficial, or even more beneficial, than taking the capsules."

His view jibes with that of the majority of the cardiologists and internists I've talked to. They are still not convinced that omega-3, in capsule form, has undergone the rigorous testing necessary to prove its safety. That it is sold over the counter troubles some doctors; they are not sure of the recommended dosage and are concerned about the pills' cholesterol content and the traces of pollutants found in some.

The manufacturers, however, evince no doubt about the medical evidence: omega-3 is helpful in preventing cardiovascular disease and other health problems. Warner Lambert, a company that has taken the responsible step of removing the cholesterol from their capsules, advises taking one or two capsules with each meal. **Three capsules** provide slightly less omega-3 than a quarter of a pound of fish, but each capsule has ten calories. That may not seem like much, but taking six a day would add 1,800 extra calories per month to your diet. Over the course of a year, that's a lot of added calories and just enough to become problematic for some people.

So questions about fish-oil capsules remain. Personally, I'm taking my lead from Dr. Harry R. Davis of the University of Chicago School of Medicine. At the American Heart Association Conference, he recommended replacing red meats with fish in the diet. Other members of the panel agreed. Perhaps the wisest words on the subject come from Dr. Bierman, who noted that eating fish, omega-3-rich or not, seems to provide some protection against heart disease. "But there is a lot we still have to learn about the entire matter." Whatever the results that research brings forward, for those of you interested in knowing which fish have omega-3 in them, and in what amounts, the following chart is a simplification of that which appears in the Appendix. I have listed the fish in descending order of omega-3 content.

Type of Fish	Omega-3 Content (in grams of omega-3 per each 100 grams of fish)
Atlantic Mackerel	2.6
King Mackerel	2.3
Albacore Tuna	2.3
Chub Mackerel	2.2
Muroaji Scad	2.1
Lake Trout	2.0
Spiny Dogfish	2.0
Pacific Herring	1.8
Atlantic Herring	1.7
Bluefin Tuna	1.6
Sablefish	1.5

Type of Fish	Omega-3 Content (in grams of omega-3 per each 100 grams of fish)
Chinook Salmon	1.5
Atlantic Sturgeon	1.5
Lake Whitefish	1.5
Anchovy	1.4
Atlantic Salmon	1.4
Sockeye Salmon	1.3
Bluefish	1.2
Mullet	1.1
Coho Salmon	1.0
Pink Salmon	1.0
Eel	.9
Greenland Halibut	.9
Rainbow Smelt	.8
Striped Bass	.8
Carp	.6
Freshwater Drum	.6
Silver Hake	.6
Striped Mullet	.6
Florida Pompano	.6
Sweet Smelt	.6
Arctic Char Trout	.6
Brook Trout	.6
Rainbow Trout	.6
Shark	.5
Brown Bullhead Catfish	.5
Pacific Halibut	.5
Pollock	.5
White Perch	.4
Common Sturgeon	.4
Walleyed Pike	.3
Grouper	.3
Atlantic Cod	.3
Channel Catfish	.3
Freshwater Bass	.3

Type of Fish	Omega-3 Content (in grams of omega-3 per each 100 grams of fish)
Flounder	.2
Haddock	.2
Red Snapper	.2
Swordfish	.2
Plaice	.2
Sole	.1
Crustaceans	
Northern Shrimp	.5
Japanese Shrimp (Prawn)	.5
Atlantic White Shrimp	.4
Blue Crab	.4
Atlantic Brown Shrimp	.3
Rock Lobster	.3
Queen Crab	.3
Dungeness Crab	.3
Alaskan King Crab	.3
Lobster	.2
Mollusks	
Conch	1.0
Short Finned Squid	.6
Pacific Oyster	.6
Blue Mussel	.5
Eastern Oyster	.4
Atlantic Squid	.4
Softshell Clams	.4
Scallops	.2
Octopus	.2

⟣ *10* ⟢

The Omega-3 Diets: A Breakthrough In Healthy Eating

A healthy diet has a goal: lifelong good nutrition. By eating a nutritious diet you can avoid harming your body through excesses and imbalances in food intake. Dr. Alexander's general comments on diet were a helpful first step toward formulating the omega-3 diet presented in this chapter. I already knew that adding the right fish to one's diet was a positive first step. But I also wanted to combine all I had learned about omega-3 with a sound nutritional program—one that would reduce health risks, provide three meals rich in omega-3 weekly, and be satisfying enough to become the basis for a lifelong program.

For help I turned to Beverly Daniel, a nutritionist at St. Vincent's Hospital-Medical Center in New York. The resulting diets afford the benefits of omega-3 while providing the means for either reducing to an ideal weight, or maintaining that weight long term. They also appeal to the palate.

The maintenance diet is isocaloric—on it, you will neither gain nor lose weight. In general, men over 18 need 2,200 to 3,000 calories per day, and women over 18 require 1,600 to 2,100 calories per day. Where an individual places within this range depends on variables like activity and metabolism. Incidentally, the first few days of these diets are higher in calories than the first few days of a diet like Pritkin's, which drastically cuts caloric intake right from the start.

The two weight loss diets are committed to steady, gradual weight loss—not the radical reductions caused by fad diets. The general principle is to take in 500 calories less than what your body normally needs to maintain its present weight. Since there are approximately 3,500 calories in each pound of your body fat, it will take about seven days to lose a pound. That's 50 pounds in a year, as long as you continue to burn off more calories than you take in.

DIETARY RECOMMENDATIONS

Ms. Daniel's general dietary recommendations, which follow here, apply to any sensible diet and help maintain a healthy body while losing weight.

- Decrease cholesterol by reducing your intake of saturated fats—those fats which are solid at room temperature—including beef and chicken fat, butter, cream, egg yolks, lard, coconut oil and palm oil. Read the labels on baked goods and processed food. Most labels will list which oils are used. The cheapest oils tend to be the most saturated and for that reason are often used in commercially prepared foods.

- Increase fiber foods and complex carbohydrates. These include raw vegetables, fruits, dried beans and peas, and whole grains such as whole wheat, rye, corn, oats and brown rice. You don't have to think of potatoes, bread and pasta as things to do without while dieting: they are fiber foods, which, as carbohydrates, release sugar into the system in even amounts. Whole-grain breads and whole-wheat pasta are the best.

- Include fish in three or more meals weekly. Buy the cold-water fish that are high in omega-3 (see previous chapter or Appendix). If you don't like fish, use walnut oil, rapeseed oil, purslane or broccoli di rape to cook with. In the following diets, you can substitute *any* fish dish for the main dish in any dinner menu. One of the low-cholesterol omega-3 capsules could be used as a supplement, if a well-balanced diet is being followed.

- Fifteen percent of your diet should be protein. This can be obtained from meat, milk, cheese, and poultry. Remember that there is also protein in dried beans, nuts, seeds, potatoes, pasta, rice and corn. Fad diets often advise high proportions of protein, but such high amounts can be dangerous to the kidneys. And, ounce for ounce, protein contains more calories than carbohydrates.

- Reduce the amount of sweets containing refined and processed sugar in your diet. Whether it is white, brown, raw, fructose or honey, sugar contains what dieticians call "empty calories." It adds little nutritional benefit to your diet.

- Limit salt and sodium intake. Avoid using salt when you cook: if guests and family crave it, put a salt shaker on the table. After you lose your taste for salt, you will better appreciate the real taste of food. Salt is the nation's leading additive—it can be found in just about every canned and processed product. Avoid monosodium glutamate (MSG) as well; it is another unhealthy additive.

- Limit the amount of alcohol you drink. Dieticians suggest no more than one or two drinks a day, because of their caloric content. In terms of cardiac fitness, most cardiologists seem to believe that one drink per day helps raise HDL levels and may thus benefit the heart.

- Eat a varied diet. Avoid fad diets that concentrate on one food, like grapefruit, or one type of food, like carbohydrate or protein diets. Unbalanced diets simply don't work.

- Limit the amount of whole-fat dairy products you eat. Use skim milk, low-fat cottage cheese and non-fat yogurt. Avoid the fruit-flavored yogurts: the addition of jams negates yogurt's health benefits.

MEAL TIMES

One final warning: if you are dieting to lose weight, try not to skip meals. Meal-skipping is invariably a prelude to overeating at the next meal you do eat. It is far better to eat smaller meals and more of them. Try having a snack between lunch and dinner, or before bedtime, but make sure that the snack is a sensible one. The omega-3 diet plan includes sensible and healthy snacks. Even when the snack is minimal, it can help you get over the deprived feeling often associated with dieting.

As far as weight loss goes, excess poundage should come off slowly. Hopefully, these diet plans will help you change your eating habits. Instead of being a chore, weight loss can become a natural extension of eating well. When I became concerned about my cardiac health, I put myself on an omega-3 diet—and experienced the added bonus of sizeable weight loss without even trying!

The Omega-3 Maintenance Diet Plan

DAY ONE

	Calories	Fat	Pro-tein	Carbo-hy-drates
Breakfast:	g	g	g	g
¾ cup of orange, grapefruit or tomato juice	90	Tr	1.5	21.8
1 bagel, warmed or toasted	165	2	6	28
1 pat of margarine or yogurt cream cheese, page 148	35	4	Tr	Tr
1 teaspoon fruit jam, preferably the kind made of fruit alone, no sugar	18.3	Tr	Tr	4.7
¾ cup skim milk	63.8	Tr	6	9
Coffee, tea, herb tea or Postum	2	0	0	.5
Breakfast Total	374.1	6	13.5	64
Lunch:	g	g	g	g
Fresh fruit: (½ small cantaloupe, 3 tablespoons fresh raspberries, 1 sliced kiwi fruit) and ½ cup low-fat cottage cheese served with watercress (or purslane leaves if available)	183.5	1.6	15.9	28.4
1 whole wheat muffin	103	1.1	4	20.9
½ cup fruit gelatin	97	Tr	1.7	23.5
Lunch Total	383.5	27	21.6	72.8
Dinner:	g	g	g	g
2 cups of bouillabaisse, page 132	1189.8	36.8	122	72.6
Mixed green salad with vinaigrette dressing	227	21.5	2.4	8.6

	Calories	Fat	Pro-tein	Carbo-hy-drates
2 chunks of French bread	174	1.8	5.4	33.3
Baked apple with apple juice and currants instead of sugar	148.2	1.4	.7	36.2
Dinner Total	1739	61.5	130.5	151.7

Snacks:	g	g	g	g
1 cup of skim milk	89	.4	8	11.9
2 slices of melba toast with yogurt cheese	37.9	.4	1.8	7.3
2 breadsticks	46	.4	1.4	9

DAY TWO

Breakfast:	g	g	g	g
¾ cup of stewed fruit compote	114	.2	.6	29.6
4 whole wheat pancakes	416	12.8	12.8	61.2
2 tablespoons of syrup	106	0	0	27.2
2 tablespoons of unsweetened applesauce	10.3	.1	.1	2.7
¾ cup skim milk	63.8	Tr	6	9
Coffee, tea, herb tea or Postum	2	0	0	.5
Breakfast Total	712.1	13.1	19.5	130.2

Lunch:	g	g	g	g
4 ounces of salmon loaf, page 147	215.1	7.8	18.5	18.2
Mixed bean salad: 1 cup chick peas, 1 cup green beans, cooked, 1 cup kidney beans. Mix with 1 tablespoon chopped chives and 2 tablespoons vinaigrette dressing. Serve on romaine lettuce.	704	25.9	32.1	94

	Calories	Fat	Pro-tein	Carbo-hy-drates
1 small pita bread	55	.7	2.4	10.8
½ cup ice milk	170	9.5	6.4	26
Lunch Total	1144.1	42.9	59.4	149
Dinner:	g	g	g	g
4 ounces of lemon-broiled chicken (1 small breast marinated in lemon juice and coated with yogurt)	212.9	4	41.3	4.6
1 ear of corn on the cob, if in season. If not, ½ cup of frozen corn kernels	96	1	3.5	22.1
6 steamed asparagus spears with 2 tablespoons of lemon juice and olive oil dressing	154	14.2	2.6	6.2
Salad of watercress or purslane and shredded carrot with one teaspoon of raisins, dressed with walnut oil or olive oil and vinegar	174.4	14.4	2.9	10.8
Fruit for dessert, apple, melon, berries or pear	122	.8	1.4	30.6
Dinner Total	759.3	34.4	48.2	74.3
Snacks:	g	g	g	g
1 cup of skim milk or buttermilk	89	.4	8	11.9
4 small crackers	56	1.6	1.2	9.2
2 vanilla wafers	34	1.2	.4	5.5
Snack Total	179	3.2	9.6	26.6

DAY THREE

	Calories	Fat	Pro-tein	Carbo-hy-drates
Breakfast:	g	g	g	g
½ grapefruit	41	.1	.5	10.8
Scrambled eggs made with one egg and two egg whites	144	8.4	14.1	2.2
1 slice of rye toast	56	.3	2.1	12.1
1 teaspoon all-fruit jelly	51	Tr	.1	13
¾ cup skim milk	63	Tr	6	9
Coffee, tea, herb tea or Postum	2	0	0	.5
Breakfast Total	357	8.8	22.8	47.6
Lunch:	g	g	g	g
Tuna salad sandwich	139	6.8	15.8	5.7
½ cup cole slaw with no-cholesterol mayonnaise	71	5.1	.5	4.9
Medium-sized segment of honeydew melon	33	.3	.8	7.7
Lunch Total	253	12.2	17.1	18.3
Dinner:	g	g	g	g
4 ounces of beef and chicken sukiyaki:				
2 ounces of lean beef strips	102	4.4	14.7	0
1 ounce of white meat chicken	47	1	9	0
½ cup sliced water chestnuts	80	.2	1.4	19
½ cup mushrooms, sliced	28	.5	2.7	4.4
¼ cup of bamboo shoots	9	.1	.9	1.7
½ cup of chopped broccoli	16	.2	1.8	3
¼ cup chopped celery	4.3	.1	.3	1.3
⅓ cup of water				
1 teaspoon vinegar	.6	0	0	.3

	Calories	Fat	Pro-tein	Carbo-hy-drates
½ teaspoon soy sauce	1.8	0	.2	.2
1 tablespoon walnut oil	124	14	0	0
Sauté the meat and vegetables in the walnut oil, add water and soy sauce and simmer for 8 minutes.				
1 cup steamed white rice	164	.2	3	36.3
Raw vegetable relishes, carrots, celery, etc.	42	.2	1.1	9.7
½ cup pineapple sorbet with 1 vanilla wafer	89	.9	.6	34.2
Dinner Total	710.7	21.8	35.9	110.9
Snacks:	g	g	g	g
2 oatmeal cookies	160	6.4	2.2	24.4
½ cup ice milk	170	9.5	6.4	26
Snack Total	330	15.9	8.6	50.4

DAY FOUR

Breakfast:	g	g	g	g
¾ cup orange, grapefruit or tomato juice	73.5	.2	.9	17.3
¾ cup grape nuts or bran flakes cereal	79.5	.5	2.7	21.2
1 slice of whole wheat bread	56	.7	2.4	11
1 pat margarine	108	12.2	.1	Tr
¾ cup skim milk	63	Tr	6	9
Coffee, tea, herb tea or Postum	2	0	0	.5
Breakfast Total	382	13.6	12.1	59

	Calories	Fat	Pro-tein	Carbo-hy-drates
Lunch:	g	g	g	g
Turkey sandwich				
3 ounces of white meat	163	5.2	27.1	0
Shredded lettuce and sliced tomato	29.7	.3	1.7	6.2
½ cup alfalfa sprouts	40	0	4	4
1 tablespoon of no-cholesterol mayonnaise	50	5	0	0
1 whole wheat pita bread pocket	55	.7	2.4	10.8
1 cup fresh fruit cocktail	74	.2	.8	19.4
Lunch Total	411.7	11.4	36	40.4
Dinner:	g	g	g	g
Stir-fried salmon with linguini, page 214	349.2	17.2	17.8	31.1
¾ cup julienned carrots and string beans, steamed and served with 1 pat of margarine or 1 tablespoon low-acidity flavored vinegar	71	4.3	1.6	8.2
1 whole wheat roll	90	1	3.5	18.3
¾ cup lemon sherbert	362	8.1	7.5	67.4
Dinner Total	872.2	30.6	30.4	125
Snacks:	g	g	g	g
2 cups plain popcorn	108	1.4	3.6	21.4
1 cup skim milk	89	.4	8	11.9
Snack Total	197	1.8	11.6	33.3

DAY FIVE

	Calories	Fat	Pro- tein	Carbo- hy- drates
Breakfast:	g	g	g	g
¾ cup apple, tomato or orange juice	34	.2	1.6	7.7
½ cup dry cereal	53	.3	1.8	14.1
1 tablespoon raisins on cereal	29	Tr	.3	7.7
1 slice of whole wheat bread	56	.7	2.4	11
¾ cup skim milk	63	Tr	6	9
Coffee, tea, herb tea or Postum	2	0	0	.5
Breakfast Total	237	1.2	12.1	50
Lunch:	g	g	g	g
Tinned sardine salad:				
4 ounces of tinned sardines, drained of oil	355	27.9	23.5	.7
¼ cup sweet onion slices marinated in low-acidity flavored vinegar, and 2 teaspoons of no-cholesterol mayonnaise				
Mix the ingredients and serve on lettuce leaves	82	3.1	2.2	11.3
1 whole wheat roll	90	1	3.5	18.3
1 pat margarine	108	12.2	.1	Tr
½ small cantaloupe	60	.2	1.4	15
Lunch Total	614	44.4	30.7	45.3
Dinner:	g	g	g	g
4 ounces of roast turkey, white and dark meat	300.1	18.7	30.8	0
1 small sweet potato, baked	114	.4	1.7	26.3

	Calories	Fat	Pro-tein	Carbo-hy-drates
½ cup of steamed vegetables, cau-liflower, string beans, broccoli or your choice	12.6	2.3	1.3	.1
1 small spinach-mushroom salad dressed with an olive oil-lemon juice vinaigrette dressing	182	14.8	6	9.9
2 sesame breadsticks	112	7.4	2.2	8.8
1 cup of fresh pineapple topped with 1 teaspoon of chopped preserved ginger	71.3	.4	2.8	18.8
Dinner Total	792	44	42.6	63.9
Snacks:	g	g	g	g
1 cup skim milk	89	.4	8	11.9
½ cup vanilla ice milk	170	9.5	6.4	26
2 breadsticks	112	7.4	2.2	8.8
Snack Total	371	17.3	16.6	46.7

DAY SIX

Breakfast:	g	g	g	g
¾ cup orange juice	90	Tr	1.5	21.8
2 buttermilk waffles or pancakes	202	6.6	6.4	29.2
2 tablespoons applesauce	10.3	.1	.1	2.7
1 cup of skim milk	89	.4	8	11.9
Coffee, tea, herb tea or Postum	2	0	0	.5
Breakfast Total	393.3	7.1	16	66.1
Lunch:	g	g	g	g
1 cup Pop's Tuna Salad, page 165	137	6.7	15.1	3
1 small tomato sliced and marinated in 1 teaspoon olive oil with chopped basil leaves	66.3	4.9	1.2	5.3

	Calories	Fat	Pro-tein	Carbo-hy-drates
2 slices of pumpernickel bread	158	.8	5.8	34
Fresh fruit, apple, pear, plum or peach	38	.1	.6	9.7
Lunch Total	399.3	12.5	22.7	52

Dinner:	g	g	g	g
4 ounces of mackerel, poached or broiled, page 155	331.3	20.7	30.5	5.3
1 cup cooked brown rice, made with half a cup of chopped mushrooms and half a cup of chopped onions	224	1.1	6.9	47.1
Tossed green salad with two tablespoons of any olive oil dressing of your choice	227	21	2.4	8.6
1 cup of fruit gelatin and 2 oatmeal cookies	354	6.4	5.6	71.4
Dinner Total	1116.3	49.7	45.4	132.4

Snacks:	g	g	g	g
1 piece of gingerbread cake	158	5.3	1.9	26
4 breadsticks	92	.8	2.8	18
1 cup skim milk	89	.4	8	11.9
Raw vegetable strips as desired: carrots, celery	45	.2	1.3	10.5
Snack Total	401	6.8	15	70

DAY SEVEN

Breakfast:	g	g	g	g
Fresh fruit: 1 orange or ½ grapefruit or 2 tangerines	46	.2	.8	11.6
1 bagel	165	2	6	28

	Calories	Fat	Pro-tein	Carbo-hy-drates
1 ounce lox	44.3	2.1	6	0
1 ounce yogurt cream cheese	15.9	.1	1.6	2.2
Slices of sweet red onion, if your taste goes that way for Sunday breakfast				
1 cup skim milk (optional)	89	.4	8	11.9
Coffee, tea, herb tea or Postum	2	0	0	.5
Breakfast Total	362.2	4.8	22.4	59.2
Lunch:	g	g	g	g
Melissa's Fish Chowder, page 128	596.4	22.5	58.3	42.3
2 chunks of French bread	58	.6	1.8	11.1
2 pats of margarine	108	12.2	.1	Tr
1 cup raspberry sorbet	144	0	.7	60.3
Lunch Total	906.4	35.3	60.9	113.7
Dinner:	g	g	g	g
3 ounces of lean flank steak, broiled	210.7	19.2	62.8	0
1 baked potato	139	.2	3.9	31.7
1 cup green vegetable, preferably broccoli	39	.5	4.7	5.1
Small tossed green salad with 2 tablespoons of olive oil-based dressing of your choice	227	21.5	2.4	8.6
½ cup fruit sorbet topped with ½ cup of berries in season	115.5	.4	.9	40.9
Dinner Total	731.2	41.8	74.7	86.3
Snacks:	g	g	g	g
Small bunch of grapes	69	1	1.3	15.7
½ cup plain no-fat yogurt	63.5	.2	6.5	8.7
3 ginger snaps (try for those not made with coconut, palm or cottonseed oil)	50	1.1	.7	9.6
Snack Total	182.5	2.3	8.5	34

The Omega-3 Women's Weight Loss Diet

DAY ONE

	Calories	Fat	Pro-tein	Carbo-hy-drates
Breakfast:	g	g	g	g
½ cup blended orange and grapefruit juice	53.8	.4	.8	12.6
¾ cup of shredded wheat	261	.6	5.8	54.6
¾ cup of skim milk	63.8	Tr	6	9
1 slice of thin rye toast	56	.3	2.1	12.1
1 teaspoon of all-fruit jelly	18.3	Tr	Tr	4.7
Coffee, tea, herb tea or Postum	2	0	0	.5
Breakfast Total	454.9	1.3	14.7	93.5
Lunch:	g	g	g	g
Seasonal fresh fruit-cottage cheese plate:				
1 cup of salad greens, lettuce, watercress	18	.3	1.3	3.5
¼ of a small canteloupe	30	.1	.7	7.5
2 tablespoons fresh raspberries	9.5	.1	.2	2.3
1 sliced kiwi fruit	32	.1	.3	8.1
½ cup low-fat cottage cheese	81.5	1.2	14	3
2 tablespoons plain non-fat yogurt	15.9	.1	1.6	2.2
1 teaspoon no-cholesterol mayonnaise	16.7	1.7	0	0
½ of a whole wheat muffin	51.5	.6	2	10.5
½ cup fruit gelatin, diet type with artificial sweetener	8	0	2	0
Lunch Total	263.1	4.2	22.1	37.1

	Calories	Fat	Pro- tein	Carbo- hy- drates
Dinner:	g	g	g	g
1 cup bouillabaisse, page 132	594.9	18.4	61	36.3
Mixed green salad:				
½ cup steamed broccoli, cooled and marinated in 1 tablespoon of low-acidity vinegar	15	.2	1.5	3.1
¼ cup bean sprouts	8.8	.1	1	1.7
Red-tipped leaf lettuce	18	.3	1.3	3.5
1 slice of French bread	58	.6	1.8	11.1
Baked apple, small, baked without sugar, but with 1 teaspoon currants and 1 teaspoon of apple juice	68.5	.6	.3	17.1
Dinner Total	763.5	20.2	66.9	72.8
Snacks:	g	g	g	g
1 cup of skim milk shaken with flavoring	89	.4	8	11.9
1 slice of melba toast	15	.2	.5	2.7
1 breadstick	23	.2	.7	4.5
Snack Total	127	.8	9.2	19.1

DAY TWO

	Calories	Fat	Pro- tein	Carbo- hy- drates
Breakfast:	g	g	g	g
½ cup of stewed fruit compote	37	.1	.4	9.7
2 thin whole wheat pancakes	208	6.4	6.4	30.6
1 tablespoon of unsweetened applesauce	5.1	0	0	1.4
1 tablespoon of low-fat cottage cheese	10.2	.1	1.8	.4

	Calories	Fat	Pro-tein	Carbo-hy-drates
¾ cup of skim milk	63.8	Tr	6	9
Coffee, tea, herb tea or Postum	2	0	0	.5
Breakfast Total	326.1	6.6	7.8	11.3

Lunch:	**g**	**g**	**g**	**g**
2 slices (2 ounces) of salmon loaf, page 147	108	3.9	9.3	9.2
1 cup of mixed bean salad:				
⅓ cup garbanzo beans (chick peas)	59.7	.8	3.4	10.1
⅓ cup cooked green beans	10.3	.1	.7	2.3
⅓ cup red kidney beans	98.3	.4	6.5	17.8
2 tablespoons of chopped chives	6	Tr	.4	1.2
1 tablespoon of vinaigrette dressing with walnut oil	93.5	10.5	0	.2
3 romaine lettuce leaves	9	.1	.6	1.8
½ medium sized pita bread	27.5	.4	1.2	5.4
½ cup of peach-flavored ice milk	170	9.5	6.4	26
Lunch Total	582.3	25.7	28.5	74

Dinner:	**g**	**g**	**g**	**g**
3 ounces of lemon-broiled chicken (½ of a chicken breast marinated in lemon juice, coated with non-fat yogurt and broiled)	166.2	3.9	28.8	4.6
1 small baked potato	114	.4	1.7	26.3
1 teaspoon of margarine	36	4.1	Tr	Tr
6 steamed asparagus spears	26	.2	2.5	5
Sauce: non-cholesterol mayonnaise	50	5	0	0
Salad made with 1 cup watercress and shredded carrot tossed with 1 tablespoon walnut oil and 1 teaspoon low-acidity vinegar plus ½ teaspoon of mustard. Blend mustard and vinegar first, then add walnut oil.	178.2	14.5	2.4	11.7

	Calories	Fat	Pro-tein	Carbo-hy-drates
2 apricots, fresh or canned, packed in water	51	.2	1	12.8
Dinner Total	621.4	28.3	36.4	60.4
Snacks:	g	g	g	g
1 cup of skim milk	89	.4	8	11.9
1 cup of plain popcorn	54	.7	1.8	10.7

DAY THREE

Breakfast:	g	g	g	g
½ grapefruit	41	.1	.5	10.8
½ cup of wheat cereal with ½ of a banana	137.5	1.6	3.5	29.7
¾ cup of skim milk	66.8	.3	6	8.9
Coffee, tea, herb tea or Postum	2	0	0	.5
Breakfast Total	247.3	2	10	49.9
Lunch:	g	g	g	g
½ cup of gazpacho soup	31.5	.8	.9	5.3
1 cup Pop's Tuna Salad, page 165	137	6.7	15.1	3
1 small rye roll	165	3.9	6.3	26.2
1 small wedge of honeydew melon	49	.5	1.2	11.5
Lunch Total	382.5	11.9	23.5	46
Dinner:	g	g	g	g
Beef and chicken sukiyaki, 3 ounces	309.5	15.4	23.3	22.4
¾ cup of cooked brown rice	133.5	.7	2.9	28.7
½ cup of pineapple sorbet	72	0	.4	30.2
Dinner Total	515	16.1	26.6	81.3

	Calories	Fat	Pro-tein	Carbo-by-drates
Snacks:	g	g	g	g
1 cup of skim milk	89	.4	8	11.9
Raw celery, carrots, cut in strips	50	.3	1.5	11.7
½ cup plain popcorn	27	.4	.9	5.4
Snack Total	371.5	1.8	13.7	87.9

DAY FOUR

	Calories	Fat	Pro-tein	Carbo-by-drates
Breakfast:	g	g	g	g
½ cup cranberry juice	81.3	.1	.1	20.6
½ cup oatmeal-pear cereal: add ½ of a small, fresh pear to cooked oatmeal cereal. Stir in 1 teaspoon chopped walnuts, ¼ teaspoon nutmeg	154.1	3.7	3.9	49.6
¾ cup of skim milk	66.8	.3	6	8.9
Coffee, tea, herb tea or Postum	2	0	0	.5
Breakfast Total	304.2	4	9.9	59
Lunch:	g	g	g	g
Turkey sandwich				
2 ounces of white meat in a pita bread pocket with shredded lettuce, 1 sliced tomato and ⅓ cup of alfalfa sprouts	226.3	3.3	27	21.3
1 tablespoon of no-cholesterol mayonnaise	50	5	0	0
Lemon gelatin desert, sugar-free	16	0	4	0
Lunch Total	292.3	8.3	31	21.3

	Calories	Fat	Pro-tein	Carbo-hy-drates
Dinner:	g	g	g	g
3½ ounces of foil-cooked salmon in yogurt, page 140	228.7	13.4	24.9	3.9
½ cup rice pilaf	122	3.5	2.5	20.3
½ cup steamed, julienned carrots	23.3	.2	.7	5.3
½ cup raw cucumber and celery strips	8	.1	.5	1.7
1 slice of whole wheat bread	56	.7	2.4	11
¾ cup fresh fruit	55.5	.2	.6	14.6
Dinner Total	496.5	18.1	31.8	57.6
Snacks:	g	g	g	g
2 whole wheat crackers	32	1.1	.7	5.5
1 tablespoon low-fat cottage cheese	10.2	.1	1.8	.4
1 cup skim milk or buttermilk	89	.4	8	11.9
Snack Total	131.2	1.6	10.5	12.3

DAY FIVE

	Calories	Fat	Pro-tein	Carbo-hy-drates
Breakfast:	g	g	g	g
1 medium-sized orange cut in segments	73	.3	1.5	18.3
3 tablespoons non-fat yogurt topped with 2 tablespoons crunchy cereal: 1 tablespoon oatmeal, 1 tablespoon bran, 1 teaspoon wheat germ, 1 tablespoon chopped dried fig	148	1.6	10.3	32
¾ cup of skim milk	63.8	Tr	6	9
Coffee, tea, herb tea or Postum	2	0	0	.5
Breakfast Total	286.8	1.9	13.3	59.8

	Calories	Fat	Pro-tein	Carbo-hy-drates
Lunch:	g	g	g	g
Tinned sardine salad: 2 ounces of sardines, drained of oil,	177.5	13.9	11.7	.3
¼ cup sweet onion rings marinated in low-acidity vinegar	16.5	.1	.6	4.1
Lettuce leaves	9	.1	.7	1.8
1 whole wheat roll and 1 pat of margarine	126	5.1	3.5	18.3
Tomato aspic: ¾ cup of tomato juice, 1 tablespoon unflavored gelatin, 1 tablespoon lemon juice, ½ teaspoon Worcestershire sauce, 1 teaspoon horseradish sauce. Sprinkle gelatin over tomato juice. Warm over low heat to dissolve gelatin. Add remaining ingredients. Chill in mold until firm.	88.3	2	13.9	10
1 small wedge cantaloupe	15	.1	.4	3.8
Lunch Total	432.3	21.3	30.8	38.3
Dinner:	g	g	g	g
Roast turkey (2 slices white breast of turkey)	218	14.7	20.1	0
½ baked acorn squash: scoop out seeds and bake with 1 teaspoon brown sugar and 1 pat margarine in cavity.	126.7	4.3	3	26
¾ cup cauliflower, steamed with ¼ cup snow peas	32.2	.3	2.9	6.5
1 cup of spinach mushroom salad with walnut oil vinaigrette dressing	227	21.6	4.6	6.9
½ cup fresh pineapple	34.6	.1	.3	9.1
Add ½ teaspoon grated fresh ginger	1.12	0	0	.2
Dinner Total	639.62	41	30.9	48.7

	Calories	Fat	Pro-tein	Carbo-by-drates
Snacks:	g	g	g	g
1 cup skim milk	89	.4	8	11.9
Raw vegetable strips: celery, carrots, sweet pepper	56	.3	1.9	12.9
Snack Total	145	.7	9.9	24.8

DAY SIX

Breakfast:	g	g	g	g
½ grapefruit	41	.1	.5	10.8
¾ cup of bran flakes with 1 teaspoon wheat germ	90.3	.8	3.5	22.6
1 slice whole wheat toast	56	.7	2.4	11
¾ cup of skim milk	66.8	.3	6	8.9
Coffee, tea, herb tea or Postum	2	0	0	.5
Breakfast Total	256.1	1.9	12.4	53.8
Lunch:	g	g	g	g
Curried chicken salad, ½ cup	127	7.5	11	3.9
3 celery stalks	8	.1	.4	2
½ tomato, sliced	22	.2	1.1	4.7
2 lettuce leaves	9	.2	.7	1.8
1 slice pumpernickel bread	79	.4	2.9	17
Fresh fruit: tangerine, plum, pear or apple	75	.2	.8	19.7
Lunch Total	210	8.6	16.9	49.1
Dinner:	g	g	g	g
Poached mackerel, 3 ounces, page 155	331.3	20.7	30.5	5.3
¾ cup cooked brown rice	133.5	.7	2.9	28.7
¾ cup steamed zucchini with dill	31.5	.2	1.9	6.9

	Calories	Fat	Pro-tein	Carbo-hy-drates
1 cup shredded salad greens with chopped red cabbage and 1 tea-spoon walnut oil vinaigrette dressing	55.7	3.8	1.7	5.4
½ cup low-calorie vanilla pudding made with skim milk	76	0	5.5	14.1
Dinner Total	628	25.4	42.5	60.4
Snacks:	g	g	g	g
1 cup skim milk	89	.4	8	11.9
½ cup plain, non-fat yogurt with half of an apple or pear cut into it	107	.7	6.7	19.6
Snack Total	196	1.1	14.7	31.5

DAY SEVEN

Breakfast:	g	g	g	g
1 orange	73	.3	1.5	18.3
½ bagel	82.5	1	3	14
1 ounce lox	44.3	2.1	6	0
1 large pat yogurt cream cheese, page 148	7.9	0	.8	1.1
¾ cup of skim milk	66.8	.3	6	8.9
Coffee, tea, herb tea or Postum	2	0	0	.5
Breakfast Total	276.5	3.7	17.3	42.8

Lunch:	g	g	g	g
1 cup Melissa's Fish Chowder, page 128	596.4	22.5	58.3	42.3
¾ cup of Waldorf salad:				
½ small apple, chopped,	29	.3	.1	7.3

	Calories	Fat	Pro-tein	Carbo-hy-drates
1 tablespoon chopped walnuts	196	19.2	4.4	4.8
4 tablespoons chopped celery	4.3	0	1	.2
5 watercress sprigs	1	Tr	.1	.2
1 tablespoon no-cholesterol mayonnaise.	50	5	0	0
Mix together and decorate with watercress				
1 small piece of French bread	58	.6	1.8	11.1
½ cup raspberry sorbet	72	0	.4	30.2
Lunch Total	1006.7	47.6	66.1	96.1
Dinner:	*g*	*g*	*g*	*g*
3 oz. lean flank steak, broiled	205.4	6.8	33.4	0
Garnish with ½ broiled tomato	16.5	.2	.8	3.5
2 broiled mushrooms	14	.3	1.4	2.2
4 asparagus spears	15.6	.1	1.5	3
1 small parslied potato	76	.1	2.1	17.1
¾ cup red cabbage salad with walnut oil vinaigrette dressing, page 00	54.5	3.7	1.5	5.3
1 cup fresh blueberries (or other berries in season)	87	.7	1	21.4
topped with 1 tablespoon no-cholesterol yogurt	7.9	0	.8	1.1
Dinner Total	271.5	11.9	42.5	53.6
Snacks:	*g*	*g*	*g*	*g*
1 cup buttermilk	88	.2	8.8	12.4
½ cup no-cholesterol yogurt with	64	.2	6.5	8.7
tangerine or peach cut in	38	.1	.6	9.7
2 breadsticks	23	.2	.7	4.5
Snack Total	213	.7	16.6	35.3

Men's Omega-3 Weight Loss Diet Plan

DAY ONE

	Calories	Fat	Pro-tein	Carbo-hy-drates
Breakfast:	g	g	g	g
½ cup blended orange and grapefruit juice	53.8	.3	.8	12.6
¾ cup shredded wheat with 1 teaspoon raisins	9.7	Tr	.1	2.6
¾ cup skim milk	66.8	.3	6	8.9
1 slice rye toast	56	.3	2.1	12
1 teaspoon all-fruit jelly	17	Tr	0	4.3
Coffee, tea, herb tea or postum	2	0	0	.5
Breakfast Total	336.3	2.1	12.6	68.2
Lunch:	g	g	g	g
Fresh fruit–cottage cheese salad:				
1 cup salad greens	18	.3	1.3	3.5
½ cantaloupe	60	.2	1.4	15
2 tablespoons fresh raspberries	9.5	.1	.2	2.3
½ cup low-fat cottage cheese	81.5	1.2	14	3.1
3 tablespoons no-cholesterol yogurt	23.8	.1	.7	1.2
1 tablespoon no-cholesterol mayonnaise	50	5	0	0
Mix together and serve on lettuce leaves.				
½ cup sugar-free fruit gelatin	8	0	2	0
Lunch Total	250.8	6.9	19.6	25.1

	Calories	Fat	Pro-tein	Carbo-hy-drates
Dinner:	g	g	g	g
1½ cups bouillabaisse, page 132	892.4	27.6	91.5	54.5
Mixed green salad	18	.3	1.3	3.5
Dressing made with 1 tablespoon olive oil, 1 teaspoon low-acidity vinegar, ½ teaspoon mustard	126.7	14.2	.2	.5
1 small dinner roll	92	2.2	2.4	15.3
Dinner Total	1129.1	44.3	95.4	73.8
Snack:	g	g	g	g
Milk shake made with 1 cup skim milk	89	.4	8	11.9
1 slice melba toast	15	.2	.5	2.7
1 breadstick	23	.2	.7	4.5
Snack Total	127	.8	9.2	19.1

DAY TWO

Breakfast:	g	g	g	g
½ cup stewed fruit compote	37	.1	.4	9.7
3 thin whole wheat pancakes	312	9.6	9.6	45.9
2 tablespoons unsweetened applesauce	10.3	.1	.1	2.7
2 tablespoons low-fat cottage cheese	20.4	.3	3.5	.7
¾ cup skim milk	66.8	.3	6	8.9
Coffee, tea, herb tea or Postum	2	0	0	.5
Breakfast Total	448.5	10.4	19.6	68.4

Men's Omega-3 Weight Loss Diet Plan

	Calories	Fat	Pro-tein	Carbo-hy-drates
Lunch:	g	g	g	g
Salmon loaf, 3 ounces, page 147	161.3	5.9	13.9	13.7
Mixed bean salad:				
⅓ cup chick peas	59.7	.8	3.4	10.1
⅓ cup cooked green beans	10.3	.1	.7	2.3
⅓ cup red kidney beans	98.3	.4	6.5	17.8
2 tablespoons chopped chives or scallions	6	Tr	.4	1.2
1 tablespoon vinaigrette dressing with walnut oil	93.5	10.5	0	.2
Mix peas, beans, chives and dressing together. Serve on lettuce leaves.	9	.2	.7	1.8
1 small pita bread	55	.8	2.4	10.8
¾ cup peach ice milk	166.5	3.5	6	28.8
Lunch Total	659.6	22.2	34	86.7
Dinner:	g	g	g	g
3 ounces lemon-broiled chicken breast:				
1 chicken breast, boned and skinned, marinated in 2 tablespoons lemon juice, coated with 2 tablespoons yogurt and broiled	164.9	1	28.7	8
1 ear of corn on the cob with 1 pat margarine	96	1	3.5	22.1
6 steamed asparagus spears	36	4.1	Tr	Tr
Salad: 1 cup watercress and shredded carrot, mixed with vinaigrette dressing made with walnut oil	89.9	4	3	12.4
2 fresh apricots	51	.2	1	12.8
Dinner Total	463.8	10.5	38.7	59.8

	Calories	Fat	Pro- tein	Carbo- hy- drates
Snacks:	g	g	g	g
1 cup buttermilk	88	.2	8.8	12.4
1 cup plain popcorn	54	.7	1.8	10.7
4 small crackers	36	1.4	.5	5
Snack Total	178	2.3	11.1	28.1

DAY THREE

	Calories	Fat	Pro- tein	Carbo- hy- drates
Breakfast:	g	g	g	g
½ grapefruit	41	.1	.5	10.8
¾ cup wheat cereal	126	1.1	3	21
½ banana	63.5	.2	.8	16.7
¾ cup skim milk	66.8	.3	6	8.9
Coffee, tea, herb tea or Postum	2	0	0	.5
Breakfast Total	299.3	1.7	10.3	57.9
Lunch:	g	g	g	g
1½ cups Pop's Tuna Salad, page 165	205.5	10.1	22.7	4.5
1 rye roll and 1 pat of margarine	165	3.9	6.3	26.2
1 large wedge of honeydew melon	49	.5	1.2	11.5
Lunch Total	455.5	18.6	30.2	42.2
Dinner:	g	g	g	g
3 ounces beef and chicken sukiyaki	309.5	15.4	23.3	22.4
1 cup steamed white rice	164	.2	3	36.3
½ cup raw vegetable strips, carrots, celery and radishes	67	.4	2.5	15.3
¾ cup pineapple sorbet	108	0	.5	45
Dinner Total	648.5	16	29.3	119

	Calories	Fat	Pro-tein	Carbo-hy-drates
Snacks:	g	g	g	g
1 cup skim milk	89	.4	8	11.9
Raw vegetables	30	.3	1.7	6.5
3 whole wheat crackers	48	1.7	1.1	8.3
1 cup plain popcorn	54	.7	1.8	10.7
Snack Total	221	3.1	12.6	37.4

DAY FOUR

Breakfast:	g	g	g	g
½ cup orange juice	55.5	.3	.9	12.9
¾ cup oatmeal-pear cereal with 3 teaspoons chopped walnuts and ½ teaspoon nutmeg added to cooked oatmeal	221	7.3	5.9	36
1 slice thin wheat bread	56	.7	2.4	11
¾ cup skim milk	66.8	.3	6	8.9
Coffee, tea, herb tea or Postum	2	0	0	.5
Breakfast Total	401.3	8.6	15.2	69.3
Lunch:	g	g	g	g
Turkey sandwich (2 ounces white meat with shredded lettuce, sliced tomato and ½ cup alfalfa sprouts in a whole wheat pita bread pocket)	226.3	7.6	24.6	10.5
2 teaspoons no-cholesterol mayonnaise	33.5	3.4	0	0
1 cup fresh fruit	74	.2	.8	19.4
Lunch Total	333.8	11.2	25.4	29.9

	Calories	Fat	Pro-tein	Carbo-hy-drates
Dinner:	g	g	g	g
4 ounces of foil-cooked salmon in yogurt, page 140	259.9	15.2	28.3	4.4
¾ cup rice pilaf	188	5.4	3.8	31.2
1½ cups sliced vegetables (carrots, cucumbers, celery, red peppers)	53.5	.5	2.6	12.1
1 small whole wheat roll	90	1	3.5	18.3
1 pat margarine	36	4.1	Tr	Tr
Sugar-free lemon gelatin desert	8	0	2	0
Dinner Total	635.4	26.2	40.2	66
Snacks:	g	g	g	g
2 whole wheat crackers	32	1.1	.7	5.5
2 tablespoons low-fat cottage cheese	20.4	.3	3.5	.8
1 cup buttermilk	88	.2	8.8	12.4
Snack Total	140.4	1.6	13	18.7

DAY FIVE

	Calories	Fat	Pro-tein	Carbo-hy-drates
Breakfast:	g	g	g	g
1 large navel orange	71	.1	1.8	17.8
1 whole wheat bagel, sliced and toasted	165	2	6	28
1 large pat yogurt cream cheese, page 148	7.9	0	.8	1.1
Coffee, tea, herb tea or Postum	2	0	0	.5
Breakfast Total	245.9	2.1	8.6	47.4

	Calories	Fat	Pro-tein	Carbo-hy-drates
Lunch:	g	g	g	g
Tinned sardine salad: 3 ounces sardines, drained of oil, with ¼ cup of sweet onion slices marinated in low-acidity vinegar, served on lettuce leaves with 2 teaspoons of no-cholesterol mayonnaise	218.5	7.6	18.5	14.7
1 whole wheat roll	90	1	3.5	18.3
1 tablespoon margarine	108	Tr	.1	12.2
¾ cup diced canteloupe	54	.2	1.2	13.5
Lunch Total	470.5	8.8	23.3	58.7
Dinner:	g	g	g	g
Roast turkey, 3 slices white meat	223	9.6	31.9	0
½ acorn squash, baked, with 1 teaspoon brown sugar and 1 pat margarine	126.7	4.3	3	26
1 cup cauliflower steamed with ¼ cup snow peas	38.3	1.1	2.7	7.7
1 cup spinach-mushroom salad with 1 tablespoon vinaigrette dressing,	85.2	4.3	5.9	7.8
¾ cup fresh pineapple, cubed, with 1 teaspoon fresh ginger grated over it	54.2	.2	.5	14.1
Dinner Total	527.4	19.5	44	56.6
Snacks:	g	g	g	g
1 cup skim milk	89	.4	8	11.9
2 breadsticks	46	.4	1.4	9
raw vegetables, celery, red pepper strips, carrot strips, radishes	89	.6	5.1	20.1

DAY SIX

	Calories	Fat	Pro-tein	Carbo-hy-drates
Breakfast:	g	g	g	g
½ grapefruit	41	.1	.5	10.8
¾ cup bran cereal sprinkled with 1 teaspoon wheat germ	90.3	.8	3.5	22.6
1 slice of whole wheat toast	56	.7	2.4	11
1 pat of margarine	36	4.1	Tr	Tr
¾ cup skim milk	66.8	.3	6	8.9
Coffee, tea, herb tea or Postum	2	0	0	.5
Breakfast Total	292.1	6	12.4	53.8
Lunch:	g	g	g	g
Curried chicken salad, ¼ cup	190.5	11.3	16.5	5.9
1 small tomato, sliced	22	.2	1.1	4.7
3 stalks of celery	8	.1	.4	2
4 small radishes	6.8	0	.4	1.4
1 slice of rye bread	56	.3	2.1	12.1
1 pat of margarine	36	4.1	Tr	Tr
Fresh fruit, tangerine, apple, plum	66	Tr	.5	17.8
Lunch Total	385.3	16	21	43.9
Dinner:	g	g	g	g
Poached mackerel, 4 ounces, page 155	331.3	20.7	30.5	5.3
1 cup of brown rice	178	.9	3.8	38.2
¾ cup steamed zucchini	21	.2	1.4	4.7
1 cup shredded salad greens with chopped red cabbage and 2 teaspoons vinaigrette dressing	86.9	7.3	1.7	5.5
¾ cup of sugar-free vanilla pudding	114	0	8.3	21.2
Dinner Total	731.2	29.1	45.7	74.9

	Calories	Fat	Pro-tein	Carbo-hy-drates
Snacks:	g	g	g	g
½ cup no-fat yogurt	63.5	.2	6.5	8.7
1 small apple	58	.6	.2	14.5
1 cup of skim milk or buttermilk	88	.2	8.8	12.4
Snack Total	209.5	1	15.5	35.6

DAY SEVEN

	Calories	Fat	Pro-tein	Carbo-hy-drates
Breakfast:	g	g	g	g
4 ounces orange juice	55.5	.3	.9	12.9
1 bagel with 2 pats of yogurt cream cheese and 1 ounce of lox	225.2	4.2	13.6	32.2
Coffee, tea, herb tea or Postum	2	0	0	.5
Breakfast Total	282.7	4.5	14.5	45.6
Lunch:	g	g	g	g
1 cup Melissa's Fish Chowder, page 128	596.4	22.5	58.3	42.3
1 2-inch piece of French bread	58	.6	1.8	11.1
¾ cup Waldorf salad made with no-cholesterol mayonnaise	280.3	24.5	5.6	12.8
½ cup raspberry sorbet	72	0	.4	30.2
Lunch Total	1006.7	47.6	66.1	96.1
Dinner	g	g	g	g
4 ounces of lean flank steak	237	7.8	38.6	0
Garnish with: 1 broiled tomato,	22	.2	1.1	4.7
3 broiled mushrooms,	28	.5	2.7	4.4
5 asparagus spears,	26	.2	2.5	5
1 medium parslied potato	76	.1	2.1	17.1

	Calories	Fat	Pro-tein	Carbo-hy-drates
1 cup of red cabbage salad with 2 teaspoons vinaigrette dressing	86.9	7.3	1.7	5.5
¾ cup fresh berries in season topped with 2 tablespoons plain no-fat yogurt. If you wish, flavor the yogurt with artificial sweetener.	57.9	.7	2.4	11.7
Dinner Total	533.8	16.8	51.1	48.4
Snacks:	g	g	g	g
1 cup skim milk	89	.4	8	11.9
½ cup no-cholesterol yogurt	63.5	.2	6.5	8.7
2 breadsticks	23	.2	.7	4.5
1 piece of fruit, tangerine, orange, apple or banana	170	.4	2.2	44.4
Snack Total	345.5	1.2	17.4	69.5

Part III

COOKING TECHNIQUES AND RECIPES

Buying, Cooking, And Serving Fish

*A*fter my coronary angioplasty, I had no choice but to take Dr. Alexander's challenge. I was determined to incorporate at least three fish meals into my weekly diet. At risk for coronary heart disease, I was quite willing to compromise on taste and variety. But I didn't want my wife, children and friends to become victims of the dreaded "Oh no! Not fish again!" syndrome. The challenge was to make each fish I cooked different and tasty enough to compete with red meat.

This was not an easy task when you consider my limitations. Cream was out. Butter, gone. Mayonnaise was forbidden and eggs, anathema. I also had to limit saturated fats as well as cholesterol.

I learned almost immediately that successfully cooking fish depends first on knowing how to buy one.

BUYING FISH

Fish is an expensive food and serving it three times a week can push your food bills up. Fortunately, there is very little waste, especially if you eat fillets. In addition, an adequate serving, both for appetite and health, is less than the amount you would eat if you had meat. But if you don't know how to buy fish, no cooking method will make it palatable. If the fish is not fresh, it will taste terrible. From the moment a fish is caught, bacteria and natural enzymes begin to break down its flesh. So it is important to learn how to recognize fresh fish.

Fresh Fish

I decided to put the problem to the fish man I have relied on for many years in Maine. "Sure our fish is fresh," he told me. "I only buy from boats that go out for one or two days. Most big boats go out for five or ten days. The fish are packed in ice as they catch them. When they're sold at the dock they aren't fresh, and by the time you buy them they're far from fresh."

"But how can I tell if a fish *is* fresh?" I asked him.

"The eyes and the gills," he said emphatically. "The eyes should be clear, not glazed or opaque. The gills should be red or pink."

I frowned at that. "But what if I'm buying a fillet? In the fish store, most of the fish is filleted, and in the supermarket it's packaged in plastic wrap."

"Here. Smell that." He thrust a fillet of Boston bluefish out at me. I took a sniff and nodded. No unpleasant or strong odor. "Go by the smell," he said as he put the fillet back on ice. There shouldn't be a strong fish smell or any bad smell to it. If I were buying from a supermarket, I'd open up the plastic wrap and take a sniff. The fish should be firm to the touch, not mushy. Hell, the market can't complain if you open the wrapping. I'm sure they don't want to sell stale fish. You know, the most important thing in buying fish is to trust the guy who's selling it. Get to know your fish man and be sure you can trust him."

I've taken his advice, and it's worked out well. I've been to the fish store often enough to be established as a "regular." Now I know when the fish come in, and I shop for fresh fish only on those days.

If you're unfamiliar with fish, ask your retailer about its fat content. Fat content largely determines the flavor, color, texture, and cooking method of any fish.

Fish are divided into three categories: low-fat or lean, moderate-fat, and high-fat. The oil of the lean fish is concentrated in the liver. Lean fish have a mild flavor and a white, or light, color. In moderate- and high-fat fish, the oil is distributed throughout the flesh. This gives them a more pronounced flavor, a firm and meat-like texture, and a darker color. And, of course, the fattiest fish are likely to have higher concentrations of omega-3.

Cook lean fish by using methods that retain or add moisture or fat, such as poaching, steaming, sautéing, baking in sauces, and steaming in soups and stews. Moderate-fat fish can be cooked by almost any method. High-fat fish are excellent broiled, grilled or baked at a high temperature.

Frozen Fish

If you can't get fresh fish there is almost always a good supply of frozen fish at the supermarket. While frozen fish lacks some of the flavor of fresh fish, it's hard for most people to notice, especially if a sauce or marinade is used in the cooking. If you purchase frozen fish, select only undamaged, solidly frozen packages. Don't buy any with discoloration, signs of drying, or a fish aroma. Take frozen fish home as quickly as possible, and place it in the freezer immediately, in its original wrapper. It is important to defrost frozen fish slowly in the refrigerator and not at room temperature, because that can cause the delicate flesh to break down and lose moisture. You can also thaw fish quickly in cool, running water. Thaw it just long enough to remove the outer coating of ice. Thaw fillets and steaks until they can be separated or cut into serving pieces.

COOKING TECHNIQUES

Although there are thousands of fish recipes, there are only a few cooking methods: broiling, grilling, baking, pan-frying, deep-frying, sautéing, poaching, steaming, or stewing. Fish can be wrapped in parchment or aluminum foil and cooked in an oven or over radiant heat on a grill, as a variant method to steaming or baking. Which method you use depends, to some extent, on the size and kind of fish, to a larger extent on the type of fish and, of course, on the recipe you want to use. For health reasons I avoid deep-frying, since the accumulation of oils in the breading negates the health values of eating the fish. Tasty it might be, but healthy, no.

But mastering methods of cooking fish will be to no avail if you overcook it. Overdone fish is a *disaster*.

Testing Doneness

Fish is naturally tender, so cook it only until the flesh turns opaque and becomes firm. Overcooked fish shrinks, toughens and dries out.

There are several methods of testing doneness when cooking fish. One method is to allow 10 minutes of cooking time for every inch at the thickest part of the fresh fish, and 20 minutes for every inch when frozen. Although useful as a general rule, this method requires discriminating application, and it's not always dependable.

I often recommend cooking until the fish flakes when tested with a fork. Flaking means the flesh breaks apart. I caution you, however, that fish continues to cook after you remove it from the heat. If it is already cooked to the point of flaking, it may become overdone in the few minutes between serving and eating.

The most reliable way to test for doneness is to cook the fish until it turns from transparent to opaque. You can check it by cutting into the center of the thickest portion. When the flesh becomes slightly opaque, remove it from the heat.

BROILING AND GRILLING

Broiling and grilling are dry-heat cooking methods that require the least fuss in preparation. Whole fish, fillets, steaks, and chunks can be broiled. Almost any fish can be cooked this way, but the high-fat, omega-3-rich varieties, such as mackerel, bluefish, mullet and tuna, are especially good broiled or grilled. All fish, especially the leaner varieties, require basting during cooking to keep them from drying out. This can be done with oil, melted butter or margarine, or an oil-based marinade.

Broiling

Broiling exposes fish to direct heat, producing an appetizing golden-brown surface. Preheat the broiler for approximately 10 minutes, then oil the broiling pan to prevent sticking. You can use a wire rack, although I prefer to line a pan with aluminum foil and oil it. Adjust the pan so the fish is 4 to 6 inches from the heat—the thicker the fish, the greater the distance. Lower the broiling pan if the fish is browning too quickly.

For broiling, fish should be ½ to 1½-inches thick. Fish pieces under ½-inch thick often overcook before they brown. Pieces of 1½-inches thick may char on the outside before they're done. Most fillets are only cooked on one side; thicker pieces and steaks may require turning.

There is an ongoing debate about bones-in/bones-out in broiling fish. Cooks favoring bones-in find the fish juicier that way, while bones-out adherents say their method is safer and less messy. There is also a difference of opinion over the fish head: leave it on or take it off? Some people feel that leaving it on makes the fish more tender, but I feel guilty when I see a fish's cooked eyes staring up at me regretfully, so I cook it with the head off.

The timing for whole fish with the bones in depends, again, on the thickness and type of fish. Generally whole fish take longer and should be 3 to 6 inches from the flame. Remember that the skin slows down the cooking time. To get around this, many cooks make horizontal gashes in the skin to allow the flesh to cook more evenly. These gashes can be stuffed with herbs to flavor the meat.

Boned whole fish can be broiled either butterflied—spread open with the flesh up and the skin down—or closed with the skin on both sides. They can be stuffed and then broiled, although stuffed fish are generally better baked.

Grilling

There's nothing quite as wonderful as freshly-caught fish that is grilled immediately. One of my happiest memories goes back to a camping trip next to a trout stream in the Catskills. I caught several trout with my bare hands by chasing them into shallow pools. Then I grilled them over an open fire. The taste was exquisite.

Recently I repeated the experience at home. Our local supermarket offers live trout that can be picked right from the tank. I bought two, rushed them home and cooked them over a charcoal grill in my back yard. Pure heaven!

Grilling fish means cooking it on a metal grill over direct heat. The heat source may be charcoal or wood, a gas flame, or an electric heating element. The charcoal should be hot, at the "white stage," and the fish should be approximately 4 inches above the coals. Try mesquite charcoal or moistened hardwood chips. These woods impart a wonderful flavor and aroma, and burn hotter than other charcoal briquets. This is an advantage because high heat seals in natural juices and flavor.

Nearly any fish or shellfish that can be broiled can be grilled. Fish with a pronounced flavor are enhanced by a smoky barbecue flavor. These include mackerel, bluefish, salmon, trout, tuna, and fish with a meat-like texture, such as swordfish and shark. The delicate flavor of flounder and sole, however, may be overwhelmed by the smoke.

BAKING

Baking is a simple, quick way to cook fish. It is ideal for stuffed whole fish. Most recipes call for baking fish in a very hot oven—400F to 450F. This shortens cooking time and seals in natural juices and flavor.

Because most fish do not have enough internal fat to keep them moist during cooking, you must protect them from dry oven heat, either by coating them with crumbs and oil, by covering them with some type of sauce, or by putting a lid on the baking dish. Fish can also be coated with plain oil. Another method, called *en papillote*—French for "in a bag"—encloses fish and seasonings in parchment or foil to seal in moisture and flavor. The result often has a steamed quality. Whole fish, fillets and steaks are all delicious cooked this way.

I have a technique of my own that combines baking and broiling—for the new cook who is unsure of timing and heat, it works very well. I prepare the fish for broiling and set the oven at broil, but I place the fish 6 to 10 inches below the flame and increase the cooking time to 15 minutes. It's particularly effective in broiling fillets that are about 1-inch thick. It gives the fish a nice toasted surface without drying it out.

It is wise to calculate baking time according to the weight of the fish. Eight to 10 minutes per pound is best. If the fish is to be stuffed, weigh the whole fish before stuffing and calculate the baking time by that weight. If the stuffing were to cook through, the fish would be over-done, so it's a good idea to stuff baked fish with a precooked stuffing.

PAN-FRYING AND SAUTÉING

If you are watching your fat and cholesterol intake, reserve pan-frying for small, whole fish. Trout are undeniably the best frying fish, but any small fish that will fit in a pan will do.

Pan-frying in the age of non-stick pans can be done with very little oil, and that can be monounsaturated or polyunsaturated. Most of my recipes suggest you use either olive oil or walnut oil for their taste and health benefits, but there are many vegetable, polyunsaturated, and no-cholesterol alternatives. Use an oil that can be heated to at least 375F without smoking.

There is a difference of opinion on the best way to pan-fry fish. Some cooks believe pan-fried foods should be coated with flour, cornstarch or bread crumbs. Coatings keep fish moist during frying and give them a delicious crispness. I actually prefer to pan-fry fish without a coating. After frying, the skin can be lifted off completely and the flesh underneath will be moist and succulent. If you like to coat fish, be aware that fish breaded too far in advance of cooking becomes soggy and sticky.

It's hard to give an exact amount of time for pan-frying. It's something you learn by feel as you go along. Assume 3 to 4 minutes to a side over a very hot fire, and cook until browned. Add more oil, if necessary. Squeeze lemon juice over fish and serve on a platter or directly from the skillet.

Sautéing

Sautéing is very like pan-frying in that it uses only a small amount of oil, but the pan should be kept in motion and the heat should be high and regular. Sautéed fish are not coated, although they may be dredged in flour to keep them dry. The fish should be at room temperature and dry, and should be turned only once during cooking. This method can be used for whole fish, fillets or steaks.

POACHING

Poaching is the term used for cooking food in liquid that *quivers* but does not bubble. It is an excellent method of cooking, particularly for the diet conscious. Very little, if any, oil is used. The poaching liquor can add flavor to bland fish, and it renders the flesh moist and tender. Firm-textured fish, such as trout, salmon and striped bass hold their shape well when poached, steamed or steeped. High-fat and soft-textured fish, such as sablefish, herring and bluefish, usually fall apart when cooked in liquid.

The poaching liquid can be a fumet, in which a few chopped vegetables have been cooked with spices and wine, fish backbones and heads, and then strained. A court bouillon, which is essentially the same as a fumet, can also be used, but without the fish parts. You can also use white wine or, if the fish is flavorful, water containing a pinch of salt.

Use an oblong fish poacher or a wide shallow pan, such as a skillet, or a heavy saucepan or pot. When poaching large whole fish, an oblong fish poacher fitted with a perforated rack is ideal. You can also use a roasting pan or large kettle.

Start small fish or fillets in almost boiling liquid, using just enough to barely cover the fish; start larger fish in cold water, bring to near boiling, and hold at a simmer. Allow 5 to 8 minutes per pound, and again, be sure that the water does not actually boil. A piece of cheesecloth wrapped around the fish makes it easy to lift out of the water after poaching and prevents the fish from disintegrating.

STEAMING

Steaming means cooking *over* boiling water, not *in* it. The fish should be placed on a rack about 2 inches above the boiling liquid in a deep pot. A steam-cooker is ideal for steaming, but any deep pan with a tight-fitting lid is satisfactory. You can improvise a steamer by setting a wire rack on empty tuna cans (tops and bottoms removed) inside the pot. Cover the pot tightly, and simmer the liquid for about 10 minutes, more or less, depending on the thickness of the fish.

Steam provides a gentle, even heat that preserves the natural juices and delicate texture of the fish. The liquid used for steaming may be plain water, or water seasoned with herbs, spices, and wine.

STEWS

A soup or stew may contain only one type of fish, but it will be more flavorful and interesting if several types are combined. Shellfish and firm-bodied fish are the best for texture and flavor. Strong-flavored fish, such as herring, anchovies and sardines should be used sparingly, if at all, because they will overpower other ingredients. It's best to add chunks of fish 10 minutes before the stew is done, adding any shellfish, shrimp, lobster or crab about 5 minutes before the end of the cooking time. Cook until pieces are firm and opaque. Serve immediately. The fish will continue to cook even after the stew has been removed from the heat.

MARINADES

The first deadly sin in cooking fish is to allow it to dry out from overcooking. Marinades help keep fish moist when broiling or steaming in aluminum foil or parchment. Sauces are heated separately and added when serving or at the table.

In most recipes, the fish should be marinated for 1 or 2 hours before cooking. Frozen fish benefit from a skim milk marinade, but almost any cooking liquid can be used. Marinades are particularly effective on bland, white fish and generally should be avoided if the fish is strongly flavored.

In an emergency—if you come home late and have very little time or inclination to fuss with preparation—a marinade can be made from any bottled salad dressing.

A FEW WORDS
ABOUT OILS

Dr. Scott Grundy of the University of Texas Health Science Center in Dallas, who has both an M.D. and a Ph.D. in biochemistry, has conclusively shown what all of Italy has long taken for granted. Among the monounsaturated oils, olive oil is particularly good for you. Formerly thought to be neutral in their effect on the blood, monounsaturated oils may actually reduce dangerous LDL cholesterol levels, while raising beneficial HDL.

In Dr. Grundy's carefully controlled study, he found that when a diet contains 40 percent fat and two-thirds of that fat is monounsaturated, blood cholesterol is lowered more than when a diet is restricted to 20 percent fat. In other words, the bad stuff was reduced while the good stuff remained unaffected. Of course, a diet of 40 percent fat has a whopping amount of calories, but the salient point is that monounsaturated fats are "good" for you.

In the recipes that follow I have usually used olive oil whenever an oil is called for. This is only partially because of its healthful aspect. The fact is, it tastes good and improves the flavor of just about every dish. There are many people, however, who feel that the flavor of olive oil is too strong. In that case, although there are many grades of olive oil and many are quite mild, any polyunsaturated cooking oil c substituted. Safflower oil is excellent and relatively tasteless, and so is sunflower oil. Corn oil is good, too.

Linseed oil, as Dr. Alexander explained, is very high in linolenic acid, an omega-3, but it has a very strong taste. Walnut oil is also very high in omega-3, and is tasty, although expensive. I use it from time to time in salad dressings when I feel extravagant. Depending on the brand, it can be strong in a pleasant way, tasting of walnuts, or very bland with hardly any taste at all.

IN PLACE OF CREAM

So many good recipes use cream to thicken sauces that a cook sticking to a healthy diet may feel very frustrated. In place of cream I use yogurt. There is a variety of brands on the market that contain *no* cholesterol. When you add yogurt to soups or sauces, be sure you don't cook it—it tends to clabber. Add it slowly, when the liquid is a few degrees below its simmering point. It works wonderfully as a thickener.

WINES TO GO WITH FISH

The cardiologists I spoke to in preparing this book all suggested that one or two drinks a day were a big help in keeping the arteries clear of cholesterol. They all warned, however, not to overdo it. Beer and wine were suggested as the best drinks, but no more than two glasses a day.

I happen to love wine. To discover which wines go well with which fish, I talked to Madeline and Emanuel Greenberg, who have written about wine for many publications, including *The New York Times Magazine*, *Harpers*, *Playboy* and *New York* magazine.

Their recommendations follow:
Salmon: a medium-bodied red wine such as a French Burgundy, a California Cabernet Sauvignon, a California Zinfandel or a Merlot.
Bluefish and other full-flavored fish: a light red wine such as a French Beaujolais, a Tuscan Chianti or an Italian Valpolicella.
Seviche: beer or champagne.
Seafood lasagna: a light white wine such as a Californian or French Chardonnay.
Sardines: a full-bodied red or white wine—a French Bordeaux, a California Cabernet, a Piedmont Barolo, or an Italian Brunello (reds); or a California white Burgundy.

Mackerel: a medium white such as a Sauvignon blanc, a Sancerre from the Loire Valley, or a Pouilly-Fuissé.

Tuna: red wines such as a Spanish Rioja, a French Beaujolais, an Italian Valpolicella, Bardolino or Chianti.

Sushi: sake or beer.

Trout: a white wine, such as an Italian Corvo, a California Sauvignon blanc, Fumé blanc or Chardonnay; a French Macon, Saint-Veran, a Pouilly-Fuissé, or an Alsatian Gewurztraminer.

⚓ *12* ⚓

Soups, Stews And Chowders

Seafood soups are an important part of the culinary heritage of island and coastal countries. Basically, soups and stews are often the same, although stews are heartier. When accompanied by a green salad and a crusty bread to soak up the broth, a stew can be turned into a feast.

Shellfish and firm-textured fish such as haddock, cod and sea bass contribute the best flavor to soups and stews. High-fat fish require more careful preparation because they can fall apart when cooked in liquid. Although soups and stews can be made from one kind of fish, they will be more flavorful and interesting if made from several types in combination.

Fish stock is the basic ingredient in many of these recipes. Quick to prepare, the liquid is made from water or a combination of water and any part of the fish, excluding gill and viscera. The shells of shrimp and lobster can be added for even richer flavor. (In a pinch, clam juice can be substituted in the recipes.) Because it freezes well, make stock in quantity by doubling or tripling the recipe. Heads and skeletons can usually be begged from your fish store.

Basic Fish Stock

1–2 lbs. fish bones, heads, tails
3 cups water
1 cup dry, white wine
1 small onion, thinly sliced
1 small leek, thinly sliced
 (optional)

1 carrot, thinly sliced
3 celery stalks, thinly sliced
1 bay leaf
2 black peppercorns
2 tablespoons vinegar

Rinse fish parts and remove gills from heads if necessary.

Place trimmings and bones in large kettle and add wine and water. Bring to a boil and gently cook 5 minutes.

Skim surface foam until liquid is clear. Reduce to simmer.

Add onion, leek, carrot, celery and bay leaf, and simmer an additional 15 minutes.

Add peppercorns and vinegar.

Strain stock in colander or sieve lined with cheesecloth. Discard bones and vegetables.

Makes approximately 3½ cups.

Melissa's Frozen Fish Stew

YIELDS .80–1.02 GRAMS OMEGA-3 PER SERVING

Some years ago, when my newly married daughter Melissa was living in Kansas, she wrote me a wistful letter about the wonderful food back East. "What I miss most of all," she wrote, "are the great fish soups you used to make. I just can't find fresh fish, except for catfish. Everything else is frozen."

My fatherly duty was plain. I adapted one of my seafood stews for frozen fish, omitting the clams, mussels and lobster I usually add. The result, nonetheless, was delicious and fragrant, and it was close to the fish stew Melissa remembered.

1 lb. shrimp, frozen if necessary
1 lb. frozen fish fillet, preferably a cold-water fish
½ lb. sea scallops (optional)
2 tablespoons olive oil
1 large onion, coarsely chopped
3 garlic cloves, minced

1 2 lb. 3 oz.-can tomatoes, crushed
1 teaspoon dried basil
½ teaspoon dried oregano
1 cup medium-sized potatoes, peeled and cut into ¾-inch cubes
¼ cup chopped parsley or dill

Partially defrost fish fillets at room temperature. Defrost shrimp in cold, running water; shell and devein. Simmer shells in 4 cups water for 20 minutes. Strain in colander or sieve lined with cheesecloth. Discard shells. You should have 3 cups of broth. If there is more, boil and reduce to 3 cups.

While shells are cooking, simmer onion and garlic in olive oil over medium heat until onion is transparent. Be careful not to brown garlic.

Cut fillets into 1-inch cubes without separating them. Put aside.

Put tomatoes in large, heavy pot. Add shrimp shell broth. Add onion, garlic, basil, oregano and potatoes. Bring to a boil, stirring gently; lower heat and simmer for 20 minutes or until fish is opaque and potatoes are cooked.

At this point the stew can be cooled and refrigerated until you are ready for final preparation.

Ten minutes before serving, bring soup to a boil and reduce heat. Add fillets; simmer 5 minutes. Add shrimp and scallops if you are using them; simmer 5 minutes more.

Garnish with parsley or dill and serve at once, with a loaf of crusty French bread. Freshly ground pepper can be added at table.

Makes 4 ample servings.

Seal Harbor Fish Chowder

YIELDS .69–1.14 GRAMS OMEGA-3 PER SERVING

Another fish stew or chowder given to me by a friend from Maine also uses frozen fish. This seems odd coming from a state where wonderful fresh fish is available, but it makes the chowder very easy to make.

2 lbs. frozen fish fillets cut into 2-inch chunks	**4 large potatoes, thinly sliced**
4 large onions, thinly sliced	**1 pint skim milk**
	½ pint yogurt

Bring 1½ quarts water to a boil. Add fish, onions and potatoes. Reduce heat and simmer 12 to 15 minutes, until the potatoes are tender. Remove from heat.

Heat milk but do not boil. Add to chowder.

After 5 minutes, add yogurt and stir to blend. Serve at once with large pilot crackers.

Makes 4 ample servings.

West Indian Fish Stew

YIELDS .85–3.74 GRAMS OMEGA-3 PER SERVING

This fish stew has a distinct West Indian flavor and calls for a few lbs. of any bland fish available at the market. The fish are soaked in a wine marinade before cooking. A friend brought the recipe back from the Islands and adapted it to stateside ingredients.

Marinade:

½ cup dry white wine
Juice of 6 lemons
¼ teaspoon or more red pepper
  flakes, to taste

2 cloves garlic, pressed

Combine ingredients.

Fish:

Marinade (see above)
*2½ lbs. fish fillets (king
  mackerel, lake trout, mullet,
  halibut, bluefish, etc.), cut
  into serving-sized pieces*
1 tablespoon olive oil
*1 small carrot, peeled and thinly
  sliced*
2 leeks, chopped
1 small potato, peeled and cubed

1 small turnip, peeled and cubed
*2 ripe tomatoes, peeled, seeded
  and chopped*
3 scallions, chopped
¼ teaspoon dried thyme
2 cloves garlic, minced
1 bay leaf
*¼ teaspoon red pepper flakes
  (optional)*
4 tablespoons tomato purée

Put fish in marinade.

Heat oil in a large, non-stick pot. Stir-fry carrot, leeks, potato, turnip and tomatoes for 2 to 3 minutes.

Add 1½ cups water to pot. Add scallions, thyme, minced garlic, bay leaf and, if you like spicy food, another ¼ teaspoon red pepper flakes. Cook for 20 minutes until all vegetables are well-done.

Strain vegetables; save solids and broth.

Heat liquid in a pot until it comes to a boil. Remove from heat, add fish fillets from marinade; cover and let sit for 5 minutes.

Meanwhile, in a food processor fitted with steel blade, process drained vegetables until completely smooth. Add tomato purée and remaining ½ cup white wine.

Serve by ladling processed purée into bowls and topping with fish fillets. Serve with French or Italian bread.

Makes 4 ample servings.

Mediterranean Fish Soup

YIELDS 2.86 GRAMS OMEGA-3 PER SERVING

Italy has given us a fine fish soup that is often served in the cities along the coast where fresh fish are always available. A variation of Italian cioppino uses 1 lb. mullet and 1 lb. bluefish fillet, though almost any mild fish can be substituted. This type of soup spices up any fish used.

2 tablespoons olive oil
1 onion, coarsely chopped
1 green pepper, cored and
*   chopped*
3 cloves garlic, minced
¼ lb. mushrooms, chopped
2 cups fish stock (see pg 127)
¼ cup distilled white vinegar
1 lemon, thinly sliced
4 tablespoons tomato paste
2 tablespoons chopped parsley
½ teaspoon dried basil

1 teaspoon dried oregano,
*   rosemary or thyme*
1 bay leaf
Pepper to taste
2 lbs. mullet and bluefish fillets,
*   cut into 2-inch pieces*
8 small clams, scrubbed and
*   rinsed*
½ lb. shrimp
8 mussels scrubbed and rinsed
*   thoroughly*

Prepare fish stock. Set aside.

Heat olive oil in a large kettle. Sauté onion, green pepper and garlic until soft. Add mushrooms, and cook another minute.

Add fish stock, 2 cups water and vinegar, and bring to a boil.

Add lemon slices, tomato paste, chopped parsley, basil, oregano, bay leaf and black pepper to taste. Simmer for 5 minutes.

Add fish fillets and clams. Simmer another 5 minutes.

Add shrimp and mussels. Cook for 5 minutes or until clams and mussels open; discard any that don't.

Serve with chunks of Italian whole wheat bread.

Makes 4 generous servings.

Bouillabaisse

YIELDS .88–1.51 GRAMS OMEGA-3 PER SERVING

This is a good imitation of the wonderful bouillabaisse served in Marseilles; in this country, the right kinds of fish cannot be found to duplicate the soup exactly.

2 tablespoons olive oil
1 large onion, finely chopped
2 cloves garlic, minced
1 small leek, finely chopped
1 stalk celery, diced
1 sweet red pepper, coarsely
    chopped
¼–½ teaspoon red pepper flakes,
    to taste
1 teaspoon loosely packed saffron
    (or turmeric, if saffron is too
    expensive)
¼ teaspoon powdered fennel seed
3 cups fish broth (see pg 127)

1 tablespoon tomato paste
¼ teaspoon thyme
½ lb. monkfish or red snapper
1 tomato, skinned, seeded and
    cubed
½ lb. halibut
½ lb. tuna or sea bass
½ lb. large shrimp, peeled and
    deveined
8 small clams
8 mussels, scrubbed and rinsed
2 tablespoons parsley, finely
    chopped
2 tablespoons Pernod

Prepare soup croutons (see below). Set aside.

Heat oil in a good-sized casserole. Add onion, garlic and leek. Cook over medium heat until onion is translucent.

Add celery, red pepper and pepper flakes. Cook for 1 minute. Add saffron or turmeric, ground fennel, fish broth, tomato paste and thyme. Cook for 10 minutes over medium heat.

While liquids are cooking, remove skin and bones from fish; cut into 1-inch cubes.

Add monkfish and tomato paste to casserole and cook 2 minutes more.

Add rest of fish and cook another minute.

Add shrimp, clams and mussels, and cook for 5 minutes.

Bring to a full boil and remove from heat. Add parsley and Pernod; serve.

Like most fish stews or soups, this should be served with crusty French bread. Serve with *rouille* (see below). Sprinkle with croutons (see below).

Makes 4 servings.

Rouille

½ cup soft white bread crumbs
¼ cup water
2 2-oz. jars sliced pimentos, drained
¼–½ teaspoon hot pepper flakes, to taste

2 to 3 cloves garlic
¼ cup olive oil
1–3 tablespoons broth from bouillabaisse

In a medium bowl, combine bread crumbs and water; let stand 5 minutes.

Squeeze crumbs dry and discard liquid. In a blender or food processor fitted with a metal blade, process pimentos, hot pepper flakes, garlic and soaked bread crumbs until smooth.

Gradually add oil until thoroughly blended.

Stir in broth just before serving. Spoon into small serving bowl. Serve separately. Rouille can be spooned onto croutons (see below) to float in soup or spooned directly into bouillabaisse.

Makes about ¾ cup.

Soup Croutons

8 slices white bread, crusts removed, each divided into 4 squares

⅛ cup olive oil
2 cloves garlic

Preheat oven to 350F. Brush bread slices lightly with oil. Place on baking or cookie sheet. Toast in oven until dry and golden brown.

Cool on rack. Rub croutons with garlic cloves.

Makes 32 croutons.

Grandpa's Fish Stew

YIELDS 1.51–2.20 GRAMS OMEGA-3 PER SERVING

Our friend Anna's grandfather spent most of his life at sea. "When he retired, he and Grandma lived on Block Island," Anna told me. "Grandpa fished all the time. I'll never forget his wonderful fish stews. There was one that took 2 days to make. I'll give you the recipe." She shook her head, smiling at the memory. "When Grandpa cleaned his catch, usually big cods, he'd cut out the cheeks and tongue, and Grandma would sauté them with herbs in milk—there was always parsley to sprinkle on top. I guess now those parts of the cod are just thrown away, but they sure were delicious!

Grandma served big pilot biscuits with this stew, and the parsley was always fresh, because she grew it herself."

3 large onions, sliced
3 lbs. of 3 different kinds of fish
  (Boston bluefish, halibut,
  monkfish, striped bass, scrod
  or any white-fleshed variety,
  using at least 2 cold-water
  fish), cut into chunks, heads
  removed

4 large boiling potatoes, peeled
  and quartered
1 cup skim milk
1 cup no-fat yogurt
Chopped parsley

First Day: Line bottom of a big stew pot with sliced onion. Place fish over onion and add 1 quart water, more if necessary, to cover fish.

Bring water to boil, then lower heat and simmer for 30 minutes. Cool at back of stove.

Remove fish from liquid and remove skin and bones. Return fish to stock and refrigerate overnight.

Second Day: Bring fish and stock to boil and add potatoes. Lower heat and simmer for 20 minutes or until potatoes are tender.

Add milk. Heat but do not boil. Blend in yogurt and garnish with parsley. Serve immediately.

Makes 6 generous servings.

Fish Matelote

YIELDS 1.29–2.12 GRAMS OF OMEGA-3 PER SERVING

Matelote is usually a fish stew in a seasoned wine sauce. I've used walnut oil in this recipe because of its high omega-3 content, but olive oil can be substituted. This matelote *is particularly good over linguini.*

1 cup fish stock (see pg 127)
2 tablespoons walnut or olive oil
½ lb. mushrooms, sliced
1 medium onion, finely chopped
1 carrot, peeled and diced
2 ribs celery, finely diced
¼ teaspoon dried thyme
½ teaspoon black peppercorns
2 cloves garlic, minced

3 tablespoons parsley, chopped
¼ lb. shrimp, peeled, deveined, shells reserved
2 tablespoons flour
1½ cups dry red wine
3 tablespoons brandy
1 lb. salmon, boned and skinless, cut into 1-inch cubes
¼ lb. bay scallops

Prepare fish stock; set aside.

Heat 1 tablespoon walnut or olive oil in large kettle. Add mushrooms and sauté over medium heat until tender, about 5 minutes.

Heat remaining tablespoon oil in a pot. Add onion, carrot, celery, thyme, peppercorns, garlic and 2 tablespoons parsley. Cook gently, stirring frequently, until onion is transparent.

Add shrimp shells. Sprinkle in flour, a little at a time, and stir well until flour is blended in.

Add wine and fish broth, stirring well to blend. Bring to a boil, then lower heat. Simmer for ½ hour.

Strain liquid through colander or sieve lined with cheesecloth. Press vegetables to remove excess liquid from pulp. Discard solids. You should have approximately 2 cups of liquid. If not, add water to make 2 cups.

Add cooked mushrooms to strained liquid. Add brandy. Bring to a boil, reduce heat and simmer for 5 minutes.

Add salmon, shrimp and scallops and simmer for 5 minutes more. Remove from heat; ladle into tureen and garnish with remaining parsley. Serve immediately.

Makes 4 servings.

Curried Salmon And Mussel Soup
YIELDS 1.32–1.78 GRAMS OMEGA-3 PER SERVING

This is an elegant version of mussel soup. For a light supper, this can be served with a salad. For a heartier dinner it can be a first course, followed by a bland pasta dish. The essential thing is to serve it at once. Prepare it up to the last step, then add the fish once guests are at the table.

2 tablespoons olive oil
2 small onions, chopped
1 cup dry, white wine
2 lbs. fresh mussels, debearded, well-rinsed
1 tablespoon cornstarch
1/4 cup skim milk
1 green bell pepper, chopped
1 sweet red bell pepper, chopped

1 clove garlic, minced
2 ripe tomatoes, peeled, seeded, and chopped
1/2–1 teaspoon curry powder, to taste
2 cups fish stock; (see above)
1 lb. salmon fillets, skinned and boned
1/4 cup yogurt

Prepare fish stock; set aside.

In large kettle, heat 1 tablespoon olive oil. Add 1 onion and simmer until translucent. Pour in wine; add mussels and cover. Steam for 5 minutes.

Drain mussels, reserving liquid. Remove mussels from shells and discard any mussels that have not opened.

Dissolve cornstarch in skim milk; set aside.

Heat remaining olive oil in saucepan. Add remaining onion, green and red bell pepper and garlic. Sauté 2 minutes. Add tomatoes. Sprinkle curry powder over vegetables to coat and gradually add cornstarch-skim milk mixture. Sauté for 2 minutes, stirring constantly.

Add mussel liquid and fish stock, and simmer 5 minutes over medium heat, stirring constantly.

Cool slightly and pour into blender or food processor fitted with metal blade; process until smooth. Return to kettle. Heat to a gentle simmer; add salmon. Simmer no more than 3 to 4 minutes. Remove from heat and whisk in yogurt. Serve at once. Garnish with garlic croutons (see above).

Makes 4 servings.

~ 13 ~

Salmon

Salmon may be one of the most perfect of fish. Its thick, distinctive flavor, its firm flesh, its moderate amounts of fat and high omega-3 content make it a prime choice for fish eaters. It can be used whole for baking or poaching, or as steaks or fillets in barbecue or for broiling. Smoked, it is transformed into pure heaven and a favorite brunch food. Salmon's distinctive pink-to-red color reflects its diet of crustaceans. Although fresh salmon is always preferred, I've included a recipe using canned salmon for convenience.

BUYING SALMON

There are a number of different kinds salmons available in the United States, but, oddly enough, our own Oregon salmon is hard to find — and expensive! Norwegian salmon is sold almost everywhere, and it's tasty and high in omega-3. So is Coho salmon, which is smaller (the size of a trout) with pink rather than red flesh. Coho salmon is usually sold boneless, and it's perfect for stuffing.

You can buy salmon fillets, almost always sold with the skin on one side, or salmon steaks with the bones in. Steaks are cheaper and have the advantage of being uniformly thick, a big help when you are broiling them. Fillets, of course, have no bones. Although convenient, their uneven thickness can cause part of the fillet to be overcooked. My fish man from Maine suggested this tip: bend the thin part of the fillet under when broiling, to make the entire slab even in thickness. It's best to take the skin off if you do this.

BROILING SALMON

While the recipes for broiled salmon that follow call for steaks, fillets can be used just as well. If a fillet is used, try to buy one of even thickness, even if it means a bit of an argument with the fish man. His point will be that someone has to buy the tail end with the thinnest meat. Your point should be, why me? If you must take the tapered fillet near the tail, bend it under to make the whole fillet of even thickness, as suggested above. Fillets with the skin on should be broiled with the skin-side down and whatever dressing is used smeared only on the top side.

My Maine fish man once sold me a beautiful, large salmon fillet for a dinner I was planning for 4 guests. When I asked his suggestion for cooking it, he said, "Cook it over charcoal. Slather it with mayonnaise, and seal it in aluminum foil."

I tried it, and although it was good, and sealing it in aluminum foil gave the salmon a tender, almost poached texture, none of the charcoal taste came through. Later, I tried putting mayonnaise on the top and broiling it over charcoal without aluminum foil. It wasn't bad. What was great was broiling it, slathered with mayonnaise, *under* broiler flame or broiler coil in an indoor stove. The mayonnaise kept the salmon moist, but did not steam it. When mayonnaise, with its egg yolks, was forbidden to me, I began searching for a good substitute. I found one called Bright Day, a cholesterol-free dressing; several other brands are also available. They usually contain soybean oil, vinegar and egg whites.

Excellent Broiled Salmon

YIELDS 2.30 TO 3.22 GRAMS OF OMEGA-3 PER SERVING

4 tablespoons low-cholesterol mayonnaise substitute	*1 teaspoon paprika*
	4 salmon steaks, 1-inch thick
1 tablespoon Dijon mustard	

Preheat broiler. Whisk mayonnaise substitute, mustard and paprika in a bowl. Smear 1 side of salmon lightly and broil about 3 inches from flame for 4 minutes.

Turn steaks and smear rest of dressing mixture on them. This coating should be a bit heavier than that on the other side. Broil for another 4 minutes.

Makes 4 servings.

Note: This dish goes very well with baked potatoes and a tossed green salad. In the old days, sour cream with dill was a great topping for baked potatoes. Use the following substitute, which will have the taste and consistency of sour cream with almost none of the cholesterol.

Baked Potato Topping

½ cup low-fat cottage cheese   *1 teaspoon chopped dill*
½ cup non-fat yogurt

Blend cottage cheese and yogurt until smooth or mix in a blender or food processor fitted with steel blade. Stir in chopped dill.

Garlic-Broiled Salmon

YIELDS 2.30 TO 4.70 GRAMS OF OMEGA-3 PER SERVING

For someone who loves garlic, this broiled salmon dish is simple, quick and delicious.

8 cloves garlic   *2 tablespoons dill (or tarragon,*
¼ cup olive oil or walnut oil   *thyme or parsley), finely*
4 salmon steaks   *chopped.*

Preheat broiler. Put garlic through a garlic press. Add garlic to oil and let marinate.

Rinse salmon steaks; pat dry.

Whisk chopped dill into oil. Spread ½ of mixture over steaks.

Grease broiling pan to prevent sticking. Broil steaks 6 inches below heat in an oven broiler. Broil 8 minutes. Turn steaks, spread with remaining garlic-oil-dill mixture on the other side and broil for an additional 6 minutes or until fish tests done.

Makes 4 servings.

Foil-Cooked Salmon In Yogurt

YIELDS 1.72 TO 2.41 GRAMS OF OMEGA-3 PER SERVING

I have used yogurt, flavored with herbs and smeared over the fish before grilling. The problem is, yogurt clabbers and separates under intense heat. It is still effective in grilling, but it is at its best in foil cooking.

The texture of fish prepared this way is not quite poached and not quite broiled, but succulent and aromatic. It's particularly good served with a rice pilaf and a green vegetable, although a vegetable side dish of lightly steamed, julienned carrots will add color to the plate.

½ cup of yogurt	*2 tablespoons of lemon juice*
1 tablespoon of Dijon mustard	*1½ lbs. salmon, steaks or fillets*
1 teaspoon dried tarragon	*Lemon slices*

Preheat oven to 400F.

Whisk yogurt, mustard, tarragon and lemon juice together until well-blended.

Place a piece of aluminum foil large enough to hold all salmon pieces on a flat work surface. You can also wrap each piece individually. Spoon yogurt mixture into center of foil. Place salmon on top of yogurt and spoon remaining mixture over salmon. Bend up sides of foil and seal into a neat air-tight package.

Place package(s) on a pan or a cookie sheet in middle of oven and cook for 15 to 20 minutes, depending on how well-done you like fish.

To serve, open foil and transfer fish to serving platter. Garnish with sliced lemon.

Makes 4 servings.

Note: Yogurt will have separated, leaving a watery residue in foil and a thin white "icing" over the fish.

Mustard-And-Dill Salmon In Foil

YIELDS 1.72 TO 2.41 GRAMS OF OMEGA-3 PER SERVING

This recipe for foil-cooked salmon is less succulent than the previous one, but stronger in taste.

5 tablespoons Dijon mustard
3 tablespoons chopped dill
2 cloves garlic put through a
 press

4 bay leaves
¼ teaspoon cayenne pepper
1–1½ lb. salmon fillet

Whisk mustard, dill, garlic, bay leaves and cayenne pepper until well blended.

Cut fillet into 4 servings. Place fillet on a square of foil and smear the top with mustard mixture. Wrap foil; seal; allow salmon to marinate in foil for at least 1 hour, but no longer than 2 hours.

Preheat oven to 400F.

Bake for 20 minutes. Cut open foil and serve.

Makes 4 servings.

Ginger-Steamed Salmon On Rice

YIELDS 1.72 TO 2.41 GRAMS OF OMEGA-3 PER SERVING

A wok is usually supplied with a wire shelf for steaming. The fish, on a plate or in a container of some sort, is put on the wire shelf. When the water at the bottom of the wok boils, the wok is covered and the fish steams. If a wok or a regular steamer is not available, one can be fashioned out of any covered pot fitted with a steamer basket. You can improvise a steamer by using a deep pot or roaster with a tight-fitting lid. Place a wire rack on empty tuna cans, with tops and bottoms removed, inside the pot or roaster. Aluminum foil is perfect for holding the fish on the rack because it can be bent to fit any shape of container. Fish should not be steamed without a plate or foil under it, for it will fall apart.

1–1½ lb. salmon fillet	*1 tablespoon light soy sauce*
4 scallions, greens and all, sliced	*1 tablespoon rice vinegar*
2-inch piece ginger root, peeled and cut into strips	*½ teaspoon sugar*
	4 cups cooked rice (see below)

Cut salmon fillet into serving pieces and place them in steamer on foil with edges crimped up to form a small container.

Mix scallions and ginger with soy sauce, vinegar and sugar, and pour evenly over each piece of fish.

Bring water in steamer to a boil; cover tightly and steam for 8 minutes.

Arrange mound of cooked rice on each serving plate. Place steamed fish on each mound and pour juices from foil over fish.

Makes 4 servings.

Cooked Rice

2½ cups water	*½ teaspoon salt*
2 tablespoons margarine	*1½ cups long-grain white rice*

In medium saucepan, combine water, margarine and salt. Bring liquid to a boil. Stir in rice. Reduce heat; cover and simmer 20 minutes or until all liquid is absorbed. Uncover; let stand 5 minutes.

Makes approximately 4½ cups.

Cold, Poached Salmon
With Green Sauce

YIELDS 2.30 TO 3.22 GRAMS OF OMEGA-3 PER ½-LB. SERVING

Both salmon fillets and steaks can be poached. Use a court bouillon; the simplest is made by cooking celery and carrots in water for ½ hour. Strain, and use the liquid for poaching.

If you don't have a poacher available, use a pot large enough to accommodate the fish without bending or distorting it. Wrap fish in cheesecloth and lower it into gently simmering bouillon. Most recipes advise 6 to 8 minutes for each lb., but this can be tricky. Go by the thickness of the steak or fillet, not by its weight. Six minutes of cooking should be allotted for each inch of thickness at the thickest part. Remove from liquid by lifting both ends of cheesecloth and allow to cool for 10 minutes at room temperature. Refrigerate until ready to be served.

Green Sauce

To be served on top of or alongside cold poached salmon.

3 teaspoons egg whites or 3
   teaspoons egg substitute
   dissolved in 2 tablespoons
   water
½ cup polyunsaturated oil
½ teaspoon sugar
1 teaspoon rice vinegar or lemon
   juice

1 teaspoon Dijon mustard
1 tablespoon chopped spinach
1 tablespoon chopped parsley
1 tablespoon chopped fresh
   tarragon

Beat the egg substitute until peaks are formed.
Add oil, 1 teaspoon at a time, beating continuously.
Add sugar, vinegar and mustard while beating.
Add chopped spinach, parsley and tarragon. Mix thoroughly.

Easy Herb Sauce

An easy sauce can be made by adding chopped herbs to a no-cholesterol mayonnaise.

¾ cup no-cholesterol mayonnaise
3 tablespoons fresh herbs, finely
     chopped

Blend all ingredients thoroughly.
Makes ¾ cup.

Horseradish Sauce

Another excellent sauce to go with poached salmon is horseradish sauce.

3 tablespoons white horseradish
½ cup yogurt

Blend ingredients thoroughly.

Stuffed Coho Salmon

YIELDS 3.22 GRAMS OF OMEGA-3 PER SERVING

Coho salmon is tender and delicate, with a pale pink color. In most fish markets it comes boned and with the skin still on. It is excellent stuffed and baked.

1 package frozen chopped spinach
1 cup cottage cheese
2 egg whites or 2 teaspoons egg
     substitute dissolved in 4
     tablespoons water
½ cup bread crumbs

¼ cup chopped fresh dill
½ teaspoon powdered thyme
½ teaspoon powdered fennel
¼ teaspoon freshly ground pepper
4 Coho salmon, cleaned and
     gutted

Preheat oven to 350F. Prepare spinach in 2 cups of water according to package directions and drain thoroughly.

In a bowl, combine cooked spinach, cottage cheese, egg whites (or egg substitute), bread crumbs, dill, thyme, fennel and pepper.

Generously oil a cookie sheet. Spread open each salmon and place skin side down. Place ¼ of stuffing in center of each salmon. Join the 2 halves together to cover stuffing. Turn each fish over so that skin side is up. Salmon should be in swimming position. If skin is not lightly coated with oil from cookie sheet, brush on a little more oil to cover.

Bake for 20 minutes.

Makes 4 servings.

Note: Skin will keep the flesh moist during baking. To eat, simply roll skin back with a fork. Accompanied by a vegetable, a green salad and crusty bread, this makes a good company meal.

Jambalaya

YIELDS 0.92 TO 1.84 GRAMS OF OMEGA-3 PER SERVING

A jambalaya is a Creole rice dish cooked with chicken, sausage, ham, shrimp or oysters. This recipe substitutes salmon for most of the authentic ingredients. Nonetheless it achieves similar flavor through a careful use of spices.

½ lb. medium-sized shrimp, shelled and deveined
1 tablespoon olive oil
1 large onion, chopped
3 cloves garlic, minced
1 green bell pepper, chopped into 1-inch squares
1 sweet red bell pepper, chopped into 1-inch squares
2 ripe tomatoes, peeled, seeded and coarsely chopped

½ teaspoon dried thyme
½ teaspoon powdered coriander seeds
½ teaspoon chili powder
¼ teaspoon freshly ground black pepper
1 cup long-grain rice
1 lb. fresh salmon fillets, cut into 1-inch cubes

Simmer shrimp shells in 2½ cups water for 20 minutes. Strain through colander or sieve lined with cheesecloth and reserve liquid. There should be at least 2 full cups. If not, add water to make up the difference.

Heat olive oil in a skillet and sauté onion, garlic, green bell pepper and red bell pepper over medium heat, until onions are transparent.

Add tomatoes, shrimp-shell broth, thyme, coriander seeds, chili powder and pepper. Bring to a boil and add rice. Reduce heat and simmer uncovered for 15 to 20 minutes or until rice is tender.

While rice is cooking, slice each shrimp in half lengthwise.

Add salmon and shrimp to rice and simmer for 5 minutes. Serve with a large tossed green salad and crisp French rolls.

Makes 4 to 6 servings.

Salmon Paté

YIELDS 0.6 TO 0.8 GRAMS OF OMEGA-3 PER 1-OZ. SERVING

One of the things I miss on any sort of a diet is a good paté to go with crackers and drinks before a meal. This recipe works well, particularly on water biscuits.

1½ teaspoons unflavored gelatin	*4 small scallions, chopped*
½ lb. soft tofu	*½ cup non-fat yogurt*
4 oz. cooked or canned salmon, without bones or skin	*2 tablespoons no-cholesterol mayonnaise*
1 small zucchini, peeled and chopped	*Large lettuce leaves*
	Lemon slices or cucumber slices

Soften gelatin in a small pan in ¼ cup cold water for 5 minutes. Heat gently until gelatin dissolves.

Drain and rinse tofu. Drain again and pat dry.

In a food processor fitted with a steel blade, process cooked salmon, gelatin mixture, tofu, chopped zucchini, scallions, yogurt and mayonnaise.

Fill a metal, 3-cup mold with processed mixture. Refrigerate for 6 hours. Unmold paté by dipping outside of mold in hot water. Invert on a bed of lettuce and garnish with lemon or cucumber slices. Serve with water biscuits as a first course at an elegant dinner.

Makes about 2½ cups.

Barbara's Salmon Loaf

YIELDS 0.38 TO 0.81 GRAMS OF OMEGA-3 PER SERVING

Canned salmon is available in every market, and it makes a pleasant and easy change from fresh salmon. The price is usually comparable to that of fresh salmon.

"When I was a kid in Minneapolis," my wife told me, "we had salmon loaf once a week. Then it was a cheap meal, but I still remember it fondly." With a little memory-searching, she turned out a delicious salmon loaf.

1 teaspoon polyunsaturated oil	*4 egg whites or 2 egg substitutes*
1 small onion, chopped	*2 tablespoons chopped parsley*
1 7½ oz. can salmon	*1 teaspoon dried tarragon*
½ cup low-fat cottage cheese	*2 dashes hot-pepper sauce*
1 cup skim milk	*1 cup bread crumbs*

Preheat oven to 350F. Heat oil in small frying pan. Add onion and sauté over medium heat until transparent.

In a food processor fitted with steel blade, process salmon, onions, cottage cheese, skim milk, egg whites (or egg replacer), parsley, tarragon, hot-pepper sauce and bread crumbs until smooth.

Grease a 7½-inch by 4-inch loaf pan. Fill with salmon mixture. Bake for 1 hour.

Makes 4 to 6 generous servings.

Note: This can be served as main course. Cold, it can be sliced as a sandwich filling for lunch.

SMOKED SALMON

Lox is one of the more magnificent forms of salmon. When it's lightly smoked and lightly salted, as in Nova Scotia smoked salmon, it can not only grace a bagel, but served alone with a wedge of lemon and a few capers, it makes a gracious appetizer.

Last summer I tried making my own lox by smoking salmon in a covered gas grill with wet chips of mesquite. Serendipitously, I forgot to marinate the salmon in salt. The result was not lox, but a very delicious smoked salmon. It was not a bit salty and the faint aroma of mesquite that clung to it was delightful. Give the fish 2 hours in the grill, but not directly over the gas, with the jets on medium or low.

Yogurt Cheese

1 pint low-fat plain yogurt

Since cream cheese is on my proscribed list, I have my lox and bagel with either cottage cheese or yogurt cheese, which is a great substitute for cream cheese.

Fill a cheesecloth square with yogurt and suspend it over a bowl in the refrigerator. Gradually the liquid part of the yogurt will separate and drip through the cheesecloth. What remains loses the sour taste of yogurt and becomes a kind of cream cheese. Makes approximately 1½ cups.

14

Wholly Mackerel

The lowly mackerel has been given bad press. My brother, who is an avid fish eater, claims that the mackerel is the most delicious fish sold. Although he may be going a bit overboard, I've tried out a few of the recipes his wife uses, and they work very well. Properly cooked, the mackerel can be succulent and delicious.

Mackerel come from a large and distinguished family of fish that includes not only the common small fish that we are familiar with, but also the yellowfin and bluefin tuna, the sailfish, the marlin and the dolphinfish (known also as mahi mahi). Available as whole fish or fillets, mackerel either have small scales or no scales at all.

Different opinions about the tastiness of the common mackerel perhaps stem from variations in when it is caught and when it is eaten. Dr. F. D. Ommaney, a British authority on fish and fisheries, says, "Nothing in the world is more delicious than a mackerel fresh out of the sea . . . and nothing drearier than the same fish after several hours on the fishmonger's slab." Others prefer the mackerel caught in spring, which is said to give a milder taste.

One thing to remember about mackerel is that the part of the fish in which the blood remains is very strong and often tastes disagreeable. When fillets or whole fish are prepared, all the blood should be washed out. If the blood is not thoroughly removed, it may darken the flesh of the fish in the areas where the blood remains, making it too strong to enjoy. The firm, white flesh adjoining it, however, will not be affected. The brown flesh is easily separated and can be discarded. Usually, it runs the length of the fish along the skin of the fillet.

Easy Broiled Mackerel

YIELDS 5.98 GRAMS OF OMEGA-3 PER SERVING

Rice goes particularly well with mackerel. This recipe, accompanied by a pilaf of rice made with chopped mushrooms, onions, green peppers and thyme, cooked in white wine and chicken broth and served with a green vegetable and a tossed green salad, can turn a plain broiled mackerel into a sumptuous treat.

3 tablespoons corn-oil margarine
3 tablespoons chopped parsley
1 tablespoon capers, chopped
Plenty of freshly ground pepper

1 large whole mackerel, about 3 lbs., with 3 diagonal slits made in the skin on each side.

Preheat broiler.

Cream margarine with chopped parsley, capers and pepper to taste. Stuff slits on one side with margarine mixture.

Grease a broiling pan and place fish with stuffed slits toward heat. Broil fish approximately 3 inches from the flame or broiler coil. Timing depends on the thickness of the entire fish. If fish is 2 inches at its thickest, broil 7 minutes on first side.

Turn fish and stuff the 3 unstuffed slits with margarine mixture. Broil for another 7 minutes.

Makes 4 servings.

Blackened Mackerel

YIELDS 5.98 GRAMS OF OMEGA-3 PER SERVING

This broiled mackerel recipe uses Dijon mustard to achieve a Creole-like effect. The result of the broiling is a blackened skin, but when the skin is peeled back the flesh is tender and succulent.

1 3-lb. whole mackerel, cleaned	**Lemon wedges**
½ cup whole seed mustard, preferably Pommery	

Smear fish with a thick layer of mustard; cover completely.

Preheat broiler. Broil fish 8 minutes on each side, 2 inches from flame. Serve with wedges of lemon.

Makes 4 servings.

Broiled Dilled Mackerel

YIELDS 5.98 GRAMS OF OMEGA-3 PER SERVING

In this recipe, the skin will prevent the flesh of the mackerel from drying out, and the dill and the onions impart a delicate flavor.

2 onions, thinly sliced	**4 mackerel fillets, with skin on 1 side**
1 cup fresh dill, snipped or finely chopped	

Preheat broiler and grease broiling pan.

Make a layer of dill and onion slices for each fillet. Place fillets, skin-side up, on onion-dill layer.

Broil for 8 minutes, 3 inches from flame.

Makes 4 servings.

Rosemary Mackerel

YIELDS 5.98 GRAMS OF OMEGA-3 PER SERVING

Some years ago my wife and I drove down the Adriatic coast of Italy from Ravenna to Pescara, near San Benedetto. We stopped at a little restaurant with outdoor tables overlooking the water of the Adriatic.

It was a beautiful day with a wonderfully blue sky and water just as blue, a day to relax and enjoy our meal. Along with a sumptuous pasta dish, I recall the fish, an exquisite pan-fried mackerel, fragrant with rosemary and garlic. Our Italian wasn't good enough to get the exact recipe from the cook, but we managed to create a close duplicate of it when we reached home. We've tried this with fresh rosemary, but somehow the dried herb gives the fish a richer taste. In Italy ours was served with the head on, but we prefer it headless.

2 whole, medium-sized mackerel or 4 small whole mackerel, cleaned and gutted	**3 tablespoons extra virgin olive oil (Tuscan olive oil is the purest and best to our taste.)**
4 tablespoons flour	**2 tablespoons dried rosemary**
Salt and pepper to taste	**2 tablespoons lemon juice**
3 cloves garlic, thinly sliced	**1 tablespoon red wine vinegar**

Rinse and dry fish. Dredge them in flour seasoned with salt and pepper.

Use a non-stick frying pan, one that has a cover large enough to hold all of the fish. Heat olive oil. Sauté garlic slices over medium heat until brown, being careful not to burn. Remove browned garlic with a slotted spoon.

Stir rosemary into oil.

Add dredged fish. Cook, turning carefully, until crisp and brown on both sides.

Add lemon juice and vinegar. Cover pan. Reduce heat to low for 10 minutes or until fish is done.

Makes 4 servings.

Mackerel in Papillote

YIELDS 5.98 GRAMS OF OMEGA-3 PER SERVING

The original of this recipe calls for Spanish mackerel, also called king mackerel, which is hard to find in the market. The Atlantic variety works just as well. If you can get Spanish mackerel, however, use it. It's a delicate and tasty fish and not nearly as "strong" as the Atlantic kind.

Papillote is cooking parchment, but I've kept the fancy name and adapted it to the more readily available aluminum foil.

4 small mackerel fillets
4 teaspoons olive oil or polyunsaturated oil for each fillet

4 teaspoons Dijon mustard
1 cup chopped parsley
2 lemons, sliced

Preheat oven to 450F. Tear off a square of aluminum foil, large enough to fold over each fillet like an envelope.

Oil foil squares well and place a fillet in the center of each, skin side down.

Brush 1 teaspoon Dijon mustard on each fillet. Top each with ¼ of parsley and surround with lemon slices.

Fold foil over each fillet and crimp edges to seal tightly. Place packages on a baking sheet and bake for 15 to 20 minutes. Open each packet and serve in foil.

Makes 4 servings.

Basic Baked Mackerel

YIELDS 5.98 GRAMS OF OMEGA-3 PER SERVING

When I first started cooking, I bought a beautiful, large mackerel and was dismayed to see my wife's face when I unwrapped it. "Oh no, not mackerel!"
"Why not?"
"It always tastes so fishy."
"Well, it's fish. What do you expect?"
But I wanted her to enjoy it, so I experimented, and came up with this recipe, which does away with the fishy taste. It earned her unqualified approval.

1 tablespoon polyunsaturated oil	**½ teaspoon dried thyme**
2 small onions, shredded	**½ teaspoon strong paprika or ⅛**
12 mushroom, shredded	**teaspoon red pepper**
2 carrots, shredded	**4 level teaspoons cornstarch**
1 cup dry, white wine	**¼ cup skim milk**
1 teaspoon dill seed	**4 small mackerel fillets**

Preheat oven to 450F.

Take 2 sheets of aluminum foil and place one on top of the other. Bend up sides to make a "pan" with walls about 2 inches high. Oil surface well.

Make a bed of shredded onions, mushrooms and carrots; add wine. Sprinkle on dill seeds, thyme and paprika. Lay fish on top of shredded vegetables.

Fold sides of foil over and seal tightly. Bake for 30 minutes.

Open foil and transfer fish to a heated serving platter, reserving vegetables and liquid.

Dissolve cornstarch in milk. In a blender or food processor fitted with metal blade, blend cooked vegetables and liquid from foil. Gradually add cornstarch solution and process until smooth.

Pour sauce into a small saucepan and cook over medium heat 1 or 2 minutes until it thickens. Pour sauce over fish and serve.

Makes 4 servings.

Basic Poached Mackerel

YIELDS 5.98 GRAMS OF OMEGA-3 PER SERVING

Poached mackerel lends itself to many sauces. Those at the end of this recipe are based on yogurt.

2 cups court bouillon	**1 tablespoon cornstarch**
4 1-inch thick mackerel steaks	**¼ cup cold skim milk**

Bring court bouillon to a boil, then lower heat to a slow simmer.

Lower steaks gently into bouillon and simmer 10 minutes. Remove steaks from bouillon and transfer to a warm plate.

Dissolve cornstarch in milk. Add to pan juices and bring to a boil. Reduce heat and simmer until thickened. Serve with or over fish.

Note: A teaspoon of capers will liven up this sauce. A touch of dry, white wine in the bouillon perks up this dish.

Makes 4 servings.

Yogurt Sauces

Any pan juice that remains after cooking fish can be boiled down and thickened with yogurt to make an easy, delicious sauce. Eliminate cornstarch and milk in the above recipe and proceed as follows.

Curried Yogurt: Add 2 tablespoons of curry powder to each cup of yogurt.

Dilled Yogurt: Add 2 tablespoons chopped dill to each cup of yogurt.

Parslied Yogurt: Add 4 tablespoons finely chopped parsley to each cup of yogurt.

Sweet And Sour Yogurt: Mix 2 tablespoons vinegar with 1 tablespoon sugar. Heat gently until sugar is dissolved. Add to 1 cup of yogurt.

Poached Mackerel In Wine

YIELDS 5.98 GRAMS OF OMEGA-3 PER SERVING

1 sweet red bell pepper
1 yellow bell pepper
1 1½–2 lb. mackerel cut into
  steaks 1-inch thick
1 bottle white table wine
2 tablespoons olive oil

2 onions, sliced paper thin
2 cloves garlic put through a
  press
4 mushrooms, sliced
4 tablespoons capers

Holding each pepper with a long fork stuck into core, toast over flame or electric burners until they are completely blackened. Under cold, running water, slip skin off and slice into strips.

Place mackerel steaks in a shallow pan. Pour in white wine to barely cover. Over medium heat bring wine to slow simmer; cook steaks for 10 minutes.

Remove steaks with a slotted spoon and place on serving plate. Cover to keep warm.

Heat oil in pan. Add onions and cook until transparent. Add garlic, mushrooms and capers. Cook over medium heat for 5 minutes until mushrooms are tender. Add pepper strips and cook 2 minutes more to barely heat peppers.

Spoon sauce on top of mackerel steaks.

Makes 4 servings.

Cold Vinegared Mackerel

YIELDS 5.98 GRAMS OF OMEGA-3 PER SERVING

This dish makes a nice summer meal. The gelatin that results when the fish is cooled should be eaten with the mackerel.

2 cups dry white wine
½ cup white distilled vinegar
2 tablespoons sugar
2 sweet onions, thinly sliced
¼ teaspoon red pepper flakes, or
    less, to taste

1 teaspoon nutmeg
1 teaspoon ground coriander seed
1 teaspoon ground cumin
4 mackerel steaks, 1-inch thick

In an enamel or non-stick pot, mix wine, vinegar and sugar. Slowly simmer over medium heat. Add onions, red pepper flakes, nutmeg, coriander and cumin. Cool for 2 minutes.

Add steaks. Cover pot and simmer for 12 minutes.

Remove from heat. Let cool in liquid. Refrigerate overnight; serve cold.

Makes 4 servings.

Stuffed Mackerel

YIELDS 5.98 GRAMS OF OMEGA-3 PER SERVING

Baked mackerel with a spinach and mushroom stuffing is a good dish to serve to company. I like to serve it with steamed, julienned carrots and parsnips, a tossed green salad and a sourdough bread stick.

1 package frozen leaf spinach
6 medium-sized mushrooms
1 large, yellow onion
2 tablespoons olive oil
1 cup unflavored bread crumbs
1 teaspoon dried thyme

½ teaspoon dried basil
½ teaspoon dried rosemary
½ cup white wine
1 3–3½ lb. mackerel, head on,
    cleaned and ready for
    stuffing

Preheat oven to 425F. Cook spinach in 2 cups of boiling water, breaking up frozen block as it cooks. Once ice has melted, cook for 5 minutes and drain. Squeeze out excess water.

Slice mushrooms and onion, and cook in 1½ tablespoons oil until onion is translucent and mushrooms wilt.

In a large bowl, combine drained spinach with onion-mushroom mixture; add bread crumbs, thyme, basil and rosemary. Mixture will be very dry. Add a little wine at a time, until mixture just binds together. It should not be loose.

Grease baking pan or rimmed cookie sheet. Fill fish with mixture; place stuffed fish upright in swimming position in baking pan or cookie sheet. Stuffing will stay in place because fish is on top of it.

Bake, allowing 10 minutes for each (unstuffed) lb. of fish. Basting with remaining wine is optional (I drink the wine).

Makes 4 to 6 servings.

15

Tuna

The Tunas—bluefin, yellowfin, albacore, skipjack or bonito—are all very elegant cousins of the mackerel. Like the mackerel they are predators, and prey upon the shoals of herring off the coast of the United States. They are probably the most beautiful hunters in the sea and are known to travel over 4,000 miles at speeds of 40 knots per hour during migration. They are also the most important commercial fish. The vast majority caught end up in cans.

Fresh tuna is very high in omega-3 and is among the most expensive fish one can buy. I saw it at a local fish store, with a sign that read "$7.00." I decided to be reckless. But after I had ordered a pound, the fish man pointed to the small-print on the sign that read "per ½ pound" Fourteen dollars a pound was too steep for me.

I have a number of good recipes for fresh tuna, but perhaps because of the price (and because it is more convenient), more people prefer canned. Fresh tuna has to be cooked very carefully to keep it from drying out. It is also a fish that is not always available in markets.

Stir-Fried Tuna And Peppers

YIELDS 1.58–1.81 GRAMS OF OMEGA-3 PER SERVING

Although best prepared in a wok, this dish is not Chinese in origin. If a wok is not available, a large frying pan will do. I like the non-stick kind because you need use very little oil. This dish is fine served over plain white rice or with a side serving of black beans.

2 tablespoons olive oil	1 teaspoon dried thyme
5 scallions, chopped	½ teaspoon dried rosemary
3 cloves garlic, minced	¼ cup rice vinegar
1 green bell pepper, cut into strips	1 large, ripe tomato, peeled, seeded, cut into strips
1 sweet red bell pepper, cut into strips	2 tablespoons capers
1 yellow bell pepper, cut into strips	1 lb. fresh tuna, cut into 1-inch cubes

Heat olive oil in wok or pan. Sauté scallions for 3 minutes. Add garlic and peppers, and stir-fry for 3 minutes.

Add thyme, rosemary, vinegar, tomato and capers. Simmer over low heat for 10 minutes, stirring occasionally. Fold in tuna strips and cook for another 4 minutes. Do not overcook tuna.

Makes 4 servings.

Broiled Tuna

YIELDS 1.58–1.81 GRAMS OF OMEGA-3 PER SERVING

Properly done, broiled tuna can be an unusual and delicious dish. The trick is to prevent it from drying out. Marinating the fish first will keep it moist. The paprika, on top of the marinade, will give a pleasing brown color to the broiled fish.

Tuna, marinated in this way, can also be broiled over charcoal. In fact, it is one of the more successful fish when done on a charcoal grill. The firm flesh does not come apart as readily as that of most other fish.

Marinade:

¼ cup olive oil
½ cup yogurt
4 tablespoons lemon juice
3 cloves garlic

1 lb. fresh tuna, cut into 1-inch
    thick steaks
½ teaspoon paprika

Mix olive oil, yogurt and lemon juice. Put garlic through press and add to marinade. Marinate tuna for at least 2 hours.

Broiling

Preheat broiler for 10 minutes. Place steaks in a pre-greased broiling pan or on oiled foil. Spread ½ of marinade on top. Broil for 5 minutes, 3 inches from flame.

Turn steaks and cover with remaining marinade. Sprinkle paprika over marinade and broil for another 5 minutes.

Makes 4 servings.

Tuna In Foil

YIELDS 1.58–1.81 GRAMS OF OMEGA-3 PER SERVING

½ cup dry, white wine
1 onion, chopped
½ teaspoon dried oregano
½ teaspoon dried tarragon

¼ teaspoon dried rosemary
1 lb. tuna cut into 4 serving-
*   sized portions, each 1-inch*
*   thick*

Preheat oven to 400F. Put wine into small saucepan; add onions, oregano, tarragon, rosemary; simmer over low heat for 30 minutes.

Place each serving of tuna on a square of aluminum foil. Pour ¼ of onion-wine mixture over tuna. Fold up foil and seal tightly. Place foil packets on cookie sheet and bake 20 minutes on middle rack of oven.

Makes 4 servings.

Note: The pan juices from this recipe can be used as the base of a delicious sauce. Pour them into a pan and add a few spoonfuls of yogurt. Heat gently, but do not boil, and serve along with fish in a gravy boat.

Tuna Seviche

YIELDS 1.58–1.81 GRAMS OF OMEGA-3 PER SERVING

This delicate South American dish traditionally made with scallops can be made with a number of different fish. It's very good with tuna. It can be served as an appetizer or, in larger amounts, as the main course of a light summer meal.

1 lb. fresh tuna, cut in thin slices
1 cup lime juice
4 scallions, chopped
1 small, ripe tomato, peeled,
    seeded and chopped
1 sweet red bell pepper, roasted,
    peeled and cut in strips, or 1
    small jar pimentos

1 tablespoon chopped, fresh
    cilantro (coriander leaves)
1 tablespoon capers

Cover tuna with lime juice in a small bowl and refrigerate for at least 3 hours. The marinade "cooks" fish by coagulating protein.

Add scallions, tomato, pepper or pimento, cilantro and capers. Stir once; refrigerate for 30 minutes.

Arrange tuna on a flat serving dish and cover with marinade.

Makes 4 servings as main course. Makes 8 to 10 servings as an appetizer.

Sautéed Tuna In Wine

YIELDS 1.58–2.81 GRAMS OF OMEGA-3 PER SERVING

In most tuna recipes, I have used a ¼ lb. standard serving; this amount will provide the recommended dosage of omega-3. Appetite, however, may demand a larger portion.

1 lb. fresh tuna, cut in 1 inch-thick steaks
1 tablespoon flour per tuna servings
2 tablespoons walnut oil or olive oil

1 cup dry, white wine
1 teaspoon dried tarragon
1 tablespoon parsley

Dry steaks and coat with flour.

Heat oil in a non-stick pan and sauté tuna for 3 minutes on 1 side or until browned. Turn steaks and add white wine. Sauté for another 3 minutes. Transfer steaks to a warm serving dish. Add tarragon to pan and reduce liquid by ½ over high heat. Spoon sauce over steaks.

Garnish with parsley and serve.

Makes 4 servings.

Herbed, Baked Tuna

YIELDS 1.58–1.81 GRAMS OF OMEGA-3 PER SERVING

This recipe is very good served hot, but it can be served cold or in a salad.

1 large onion, chopped
2 cloves garlic, minced
1 tablespoon olive oil plus 1 teaspoon for oiling baking dish
1 teaspoon thyme

½ teaspoon marjoram
½ teaspoon rosemary
½ teaspoon sweet basil
1 cup dry, white wine
1 lb. fresh tuna cut in 1 inch-thick steaks

Sauté onion and garlic in olive oil until soft but not browned.

Add thyme, marjoram, rosemary, sweet basil and wine. Remove from heat after wine is added.

Preheat oven to 350F.

Oil bottom of a baking dish. Place tuna in dish and pour wine-herb mixture over each portion.

Bake for 30 minutes or until fish flakes easily when tested with fork.

Makes 4 servings.

My Father's Tuna Salad

YIELDS 1.47–1.70 GRAMS OF OMEGA-3 PER SERVING

I grew up in an all-male household in the '30s. My father did the cooking when he was able to, and the rest of the time my brothers and I managed. We had Pop's favorite dish, tuna fish salad, at least three nights every week. In those Depression days, it was economical. Had we known how important omega-3 was, we probably wouldn't have grumbled.

I still love a tuna salad made this way. I'm fairly sure Dad added lettuce to the salad to stretch 1 can of tuna into a meal for himself and three hungry boys. Nonetheless, it was an inspired idea. I've served it to my own children, and they love it. It lightens the salad, and if the lettuce is crisp and crunchy, it's a perfect counterpoint to the celery. The light touch of mayonnaise doesn't overwhelm the taste of the tuna. I've modified my father's recipe to make it more healthy for the heart.

*2 7½-oz. cans white tuna,
    preferably albacore, packed
    in oil
2 stalks celery, diced
2 scallions, diced*

*¼ head iceberg lettuce
2 tablespoons no-cholesterol
    mayonnaise
4 large lettuce-leaf cups*

Rinse tuna with vinegar to remove oil.

In a large bowl, combine celery and scallions. Dice lettuce, and add to bowl. Add tuna and mayonnaise. Mix thoroughly, breaking tuna into small pieces, but do not mash.

Serve in lettuce-leaf cups.

Makes 4 servings.

Bombay Curried Tuna

YIELDS .98–1.70 GRAMS OF OMEGA-3 PER SERVING

Canned tuna lends itself well to curry. I make my own curry sauce, which is not very difficult. All of the spices are generally available in supermarkets, and most of us have them on our spice racks. Instead of the clarified butter of Indian recipes, I use corn-oil margarine, which has the least amount of saturated fat.

2 tablespoons corn-oil margarine
1 large onion, chopped
1 Granny Smith apple, cored and
    chopped
1 teaspoon ground ginger
1 teaspoon turmeric
½ teaspoon cayenne pepper
½ teaspoon ground cinnamon

½ teaspoon ground coriander
    seed
1 teaspoon mustard powder
1 teaspoon ground cumin
½ cup dry, white wine
1 cup tomato purée
2 7½-oz. cans white, oil-packed
    tuna, drained

Condiments:

Chopped walnuts
Chopped green onions
Dry-roasted peanuts
Raisins

Chutney
Diced apples
Dried bananas
Chopped crystallized ginger

Heat margarine in large frying pan over medium heat.

Sauté onion and apple until onion is transparent.

Add spices, one at a time, stirring well after each addition.

Add white wine and tomato purée. Simmer 5 minutes.

Add tuna fish, and break up pieces with wooden spoon. Mix thoroughly, and serve.

Makes 4 to 6 servings when accompanied by white rice and choice of condiments in small side dishes.

Tuna Plate

YIELDS 1.47–1.70 GRAMS OF OMEGA-3 PER SERVING

One of my favorite ways of eating canned tuna is also the easiest way to serve it. It's good for those nights when you get home too tired to do anything. Just serve and relax.

1 7½-oz. can white or dark, oil-
** packed tuna, drained**
2 tablespoons low-acidity vinegar
2 head-lettuce leaves

Chilled, raw vegetables (carrots,
** celery, radishes, scallions,**
** etc.), cut into sticks or**
** finger-sized pieces**

Rinse tuna with vinegar. Arrange ½ can on each lettuce leaf. Surround with chilled raw vegetable strips.

Makes 2 servings and should be served with bread and a good, dry white wine.

Tuna Pasta Casserole

YIELDS .49–.57 GRAMS OF OMEGA-3 PER SERVING

When our kids were young, one of their favorite dishes was a tuna-noodle casserole. I've adapted that early version by using pasta instead of egg noodles and a sauce that has virtually no cholesterol.

2 bouillon cubes
1 cup hot water
½ cup cottage cheese
2 tablespoons chopped, fresh dill
½ lb. elbow macaroni

1 teaspoon polyunsaturated oil
1 7½-oz. can tuna
¼ cup unflavored bread crumbs
1 tablespoon chopped, fresh
** parsley**

Dissolve bouillon in hot water, blending in cottage cheese and dill.

Cook noodles according to package directions, or *al dente*, i.e. firm but not too soft.

Preheat oven to 450F. Grease a medium-sized casserole with oil. Combine cooked macaroni, tuna and sauce in casserole. Top with a thin layer of bread crumbs mixed with parsley. Bake for 45 minutes.

Makes 6 servings.

SUSHI

One easy way to enjoy fresh tuna is in the Japanese dish, *sushi*. In its basic form, it is a thin sliver of raw fish on top of a mound of vinegared rice. The "raw" usually stops most people in their tracks. Good, fresh sushi has no fishy taste, is delectable and is usually presented in a striking manner.

The key, of course, is the word fresh. The fish must be absolutely fresh, and for that reason no fish bought in the usual market will qualify.

Every once in a while, however, exceptionally fresh tuna will be available, advertised as "for sushi." That's when I buy it and make my own sushi. At other times I have to be content to get my "sushi-fix" at the nearest sushi bar.

A good sushi bar will have a great assortment of different tuna sushi available. There is *maguro*, plain tuna, and *toro*, fatty tuna belly; *shiro maguro* (albacore tuna), *hamachi* (yellowtail, which is the amberjack, a fish similar to the tuna), and *katsuo*—bonito or skipjack.

But there are also many types of sushi that aren't tuna. There is *kohoda*, the Japanese shad, and our old friend the mackerel, in Japanese, *saba*. There is *sake* (salmon), *tai* (red snapper), *hirame* (halibut), *suzuki* (sea bass) and so on.

The true sushi lover tastes them all, but as to making them into sushi at home, the only market fish I use is tuna that a trustworthy fish man assures me is fresh enough for sushi. Of course, if you are a fisherman or live near the docks where the boats come in, you can make your own sushi from almost any freshly caught fish.

The only problem with sushi as a source of omega-3 is the small amount of fish used. To get one-fourth of a pound, you will have to eat quite a bit, but once you are hooked this should be no problem!

First, however, there is the vinegared rice. You must use short-grained rice, which sticks together nicely.

Vinegared Rice

2 cups rice
2 cups water
1 teaspoon salt

1 tablespoon sugar
¼ cup rice vinegar

Rinse rice until water runs clear.

Add water. Bring to a boil, stirring from time to time. Cover pot and reduce heat to a very low simmer. Cook for 20 minutes.

Mix salt, sugar and vinegar in a small bowl and stir until sugar is dissolved.

When rice is done, drain it thoroughly, and put it into a glass, ceramic or wooden bowl. Add vinegar solution, 1 tablespoon at a time. If the rice is fanned as it cools, it will become glossy. It doesn't change the taste, but it looks nice, and appearance is an important aspect of Japanese cuisine.

Sushi

YIELDS .11 GRAMS OF OMEGA-3 PER PIECE

I sometimes think Americans eat sushi for the wasabi—*Japanese horse-radish. You can buy it in powdered form in any oriental food store. It comes in a small can, and you simply add a few drops of water to some powder to make a paste.*

Vinegared rice (see above)
Small piece of very fresh tuna
    (¼ lb. goes a long way
    with sushi)
Wasabi

Prepare rice pads. Put a few tablespoons of cooked, vinegared rice in one hand and press it into an oval shape using the first 2 fingers of your other hand.

Slice tuna into ¼-inch thick slices. Each slice should be approximately 1½ inches long and ½ inch wide.

Smear a touch of *wasabi* on top of rice oval. Place slice of tuna over *wasabi*. You've made your first sushi! This type is called *nigirizushi*.

Once you become adept at this, you can branch out and explore other types of sushi, such as *makizushi*, a roll with seaweed on the outside and rice and fish or vegetables inside. If you like sushi, there are many good books devoted to its preparation, including the decorative and slightly mystical aspects involved.

Note: It is very difficult to say just what a serving of sushi is. As an appetizer before the meal, 3 or 4 slices on rice pads should do. For a whole meal, you need about 7 or 8 slices, depending on your appetite. Slivered, pickled ginger, which can be found in most Oriental markets, is a perfect accompaniment to sushi.

⚊ *16* ⚊

Bluefish

---

*B*luefish means different things to different people. I have heard it described as oily and robustly flavored by one food writer, as so delicate in flavor that it needs only light seasonings to enhance it, by another. I had always been uncertain about it, often finding its flavor too strong and "fishy" for my taste. Then, one summer in Maine, I arrived late at my fish retailer's truck and found that he had only bluefish left. When I hesitated, he said, "These are Boston blues. Try them."

I did and was genuinely surprised. The flesh was white and delicate, the taste subtle and very pleasing. The next week I asked him why his blues were so much better than any other. "Are Boston blues a different fish?" I asked.

"It's not that," he assured me. "It's just that my fish are fresh. That's the big difference."

Taking him at his word, I began to pay particular attention to the freshness of bluefish: when I found a genuinely fresh blue it was as if I had encountered a different species. I began to understand the popularity of this fish among people who live near the sea. Freshly caught and cooked, bluefish is superb. Unfortunately, because it is a very oily fish, it freezes poorly. On the other hand, it is spectacular when smoked. As an added bonus, it is high in omega-3.

Bluefish fillets have a strip of dark flesh running down the center that has a strong fishy flavor. To remove, cut a shallow V along both sides of the dark strip, being careful not to cut completely through the flesh. Lift the strip out and discard it.

Broiled Whole Bluefish

YIELDS 2.72 TO 2.78 GRAMS OF OMEGA-3 PER SERVING

With any good-tasting fish, broiling is one of the best methods of cooking, and blues take well to broiling. Here is one of the simplest and easiest methods.

1 whole bluefish, 3–4 lbs., cleaned, rinsed and dried	*2 teaspoons dried oregano*
1 teaspoon olive or walnut oil	*3 teaspoons fresh parsley, chopped very fine*
2 lemons, cut in wedges	

Oil fish very lightly. Make 4 diagonal slashes in flesh on each side, down to the bone.

Mix oregano and parsley together on a small plate. Dip lemon wedges in herb mixture to coat and place a wedge in each slash.

Broil fish, 5 minutes to a side, 4 to 5 inches under a preheated gas or electric broiler, or grill over charcoal. The timing will vary slightly, depending on size of fish. Test fish by flaking with a fork.

Makes 4 servings.

Plain Broiled Bluefish

YIELDS 2.72 GRAMS OF OMEGA-3 PER SERVING

Another method of broiling bluefish whole does away with the gashes. The skin, uncut, keeps the flesh moist and succulent.

1 whole bluefish, 3–4 lbs., cleaned and dried	*1 tablespoon lemon juice*
2 tablespoons olive oil	*1 tablespoon fresh parsley, finely chopped*
2 tablespoons flour	*4 or 5 sprigs parsley*

Oil fish with ½ tablespoon oil. Coat entire fish with a thin layer of flour. Allow to sit about 10 minutes. In the meantime, preheat broiler.

Broil about 3 to 4 inches from flame for about 4 to 5 minutes to a side, more if fish is thicker than 2 inches.

Combine remaining olive oil with lemon juice and parsley, and whisk thoroughly.

To serve, remove skin carefully from 1 side of fish and transfer, including bone, to serving platter. Pour parsley sauce over fish and garnish with parsley sprigs.

Makes 4 servings.

Broiled Bluefish Flambé

YIELDS 2.72 GRAMS OF OMEGA-3 PER SERVING

This is a simple but rather impressive way of serving broiled bluefish. My wife tried it many years ago when we had a house on Shelter Island near the eastern end of Long Island. Our neighbor was a dedicated fisherman and brought home much more than he could possibly use himself. He would always give us some of his catch, and, while we were grateful, we soon began to be sick of fish, especially when the blues were running. After the tenth day in a row, my kids rebelled: "No more bluefish!" My wife gave them scrambled eggs for supper and prepared the day's gift just for the two of us, flambé. Naturally the kids were enchanted when it came to the table flaming. They insisted on "just tasting it"; they ate most of it.

½ cup fresh fennel, chopped	4 good-sized bluefish fillets,
½ cup fresh parsley, chopped	skin on
1 tablespoon dried thyme	½ teaspoon paprika
	¼ cup brandy

Preheat broiler. Mix fennel, parsley and thyme. Place fish fillets, skin side down, on oiled broiling pan. Sprinkle on paprika and then evenly place mixed herbs over fillets.

Broil 5 minutes about 3 inches from flame.

Remove fillets from pan and place on a fireproof serving dish. Warm brandy over stove, carefully; pour it over fillets and ignite. Carry flaming platter to table.

Makes 4 servings.

Note: Do not use glass serving plates: the flame's heat can cause them to crack. Wear gloves because the plate becomes very hot as brandy flames.

Bluefish Broiled On Fennel

YIELDS 2.72 GRAMS OF OMEGA-3 PER SERVING

Fennel, with its licorice-like flavor, complements the taste of bluefish.

2 fennel bulbs, chopped   **4 bluefish fillets**
1 teaspoon fennel seeds

Simmer fennel bulbs in water for 15 minutes; drain.

Put cooked fennel in a layer at bottom of broiling pan; place fillets on top, skin-side up.

Broil as close to flame as possible. Skin will protect flesh. Broil 10 minutes.

Turn fillets and sprinkle fennel seeds over top. Broil another minute to brown.

Makes 4 servings

Stuffed Baked Bluefish

YIELDS 2.91 GRAMS OF OMEGA-3 PER SERVING

This is a wonderful recipe, not only in terms of taste, but because the stuffing increases the amount of omega-3 in the dish. The imitation crabmeat is sometimes sold as Sealegs™, a trademark for a mixture of pollock, crabmeat, starch, egg whites and spices.

½ cup low-fat cottage cheese   **1 cup imitation crabmeat**
¼ cup tofu   **1 medium-sized bluefish, cleaned,**
¼ cup bread crumbs   **scaled**
1 teaspoon dried thyme   **1 tablespoon polyunsaturated oil**
1 tablespoon chopped fresh dill   **(any kind)**
1 tablespoon chopped parsley   **Lemon wedges**

Preheat oven to 425F. Combine cottage cheese and tofu in food processor fitted with steel blade and process until well-mixed, but not too smooth.

Pour tofu-cottage cheese mix into large bowl; add bread crumbs, spices and imitation crabmeat. Mix thoroughly.

Rinse fish inside and out; pat dry with paper towels. Fill bluefish with stuffing mixture and close opening with steel skewers or wooden picks, or sew it closed.

Oil outside of fish and bake uncovered for 8 to 10 minutes per inch of thickness or until fish tests done. Serve with lemon wedges.

Makes 4 servings.

Apple Baked Bluefish

YIELDS 2.72 TO 2.91 GRAMS OF OMEGA-3 PER SERVING

The mayonnaise-mustard mixture used in this recipe seems to take away the strong taste of bluefish.

2 Granny Smith apples	*4 tablespoons no-cholesterol*
1 tablespoon walnut oil or any	*mayonnaise*
mild, poyunsaturated oil	*3 tablespoons chopped chives*
2 large bluefish fillets	*2 cups dry, white wine*
4 tablespoons Dijon mustard	*¼ cup non-fat yogurt*

Preheat oven to 350F. Core apples and cut into thin wedges. Sauté apples in oil until lightly browned.

Put bluefish fillets into shallow baking dish, skin-side down, and spread apples around and over fish.

Mix mustard, mayonnaise and chives together; spread evenly over fillets.

Pour about 1 cup wine in and around fillets. Wine should only come halfway up fillets. Do not wash off mustard-mayonnaise coating.

Bake for 20 to 25 minutes.

Remove fish from pan to a serving dish; keep warm. Drain liquid into pot and add remaining wine. Reduce by ½ over high heat. Remove from stove and allow to cool slightly. Whisk in ¼ cup yogurt until smooth.

Pour sauce over fish and serve immediately.

Makes 4 servings.

Gin-Fired Bluefish

YIELDS 2.72 GRAMS OF OMEGA-3 PER SERVING

This recipe cooks the bluefish in foil with a mixture of spices. Flaming with gin, according to the Shelter Islander who introduced me to this method, dates back to prohibition. "We had plenty of gin around the island, then. Bad gin, but plenty of it!"

1 tablespoon olive oil	*2 tablespoons fresh dill, chopped*
2 large bluefish fillets	*1 teaspoon dried rosemary*
½ teaspoon paprika	*½ cup gin*

Preheat broiler. Oil fillets and place on broiling pan, skin-side down. Sprinkle surface with paprika. Broil 3 inches from flame for 5 minutes. After 5 minutes, check to see if flesh has become opaque. If not, continue broiling.

Remove fillets from pan and place on a serving dish. Sprinkle with dill and rosemary.

Heat gin in small pan; ignite; pour over fillets. When gin burns off, serve at once. A subtle flavoring of dill and rosemary will be transmitted to fish by the burning gin.

Bluefish In White Wine

YIELDS 2.91 GRAMS OF OMEGA-3 PER SERVING

This was another Shelter Island favorite. It can be baked in the oven or outdoors over charcoal and is excellent served hot over rice. It has a pleasant sweet-and-sour taste and is also good cold as an appetizer.

2 cloves garlic, minced	*1 cup dry, white wine*
1 medium onion, sliced	*¼ cup vinegar*
1 tablespoon walnut oil	*¼ cup sugar*
½ teaspoon dried tarragon	*4 small bluefish fillets*

Preheat oven to 350F. In a small pan, cook garlic and onion in walnut oil until onion is transparent.

Add tarragon, white wine, vinegar and sugar, and simmer at a low heat for about 20 minutes.

Place fillets on a large square of aluminum foil, skin-side down, and cover with sauce. Bring ends and sides of foil up to form a tight envelope.

Bake in oven for 20 minutes or over charcoal for the same amount of time, turning every 5 minutes.

Makes 4 servings.

17

Trout

The first time I tasted blue trout was in Germany, in the town of Freiburg near the Black Forest. My wife and I ate it at an outdoor restaurant. I still remember the combination of the trees around us, the sound of a nearby stream and the lovely color of the fish, and always associate that time with the taste of blue trout.

Trout, no matter how it is cooked, is a delectable fish. It can be broiled, baked, pan-fried, barbecued, poached, steamed or sautéed. Once cooked, the trout meat is white and firm, but it flakes easily. Trout can be cooked with or without the heads, but the skin should be left on. Broiled or pan-fried trout end up with a tasty, edible skin. Brook and rainbow trout don't have scales and are easy to clean.

The trout for sale in the markets is almost always from Idaho and reasonably fresh. Trout has delicate skin that damages easily. Trout should be bought live and chosen right from the fish tank. Tell the fish man to eviscerate them with as little handling as possible.

SMOKED TROUT

Trout lends itself to smoking, and once smoked it can be kept, refrigerated, for at least a week. It's a fine Sunday brunch food served with coffee and toasted, sliced bagels. I smoke trout in a propane gas grill. The grill usually comes with a rack that fits above the gas jets and volcanic rock and another shelf-like grill farther up. A charcoal grill, however, will work, too. Just be sure you have enough charcoal to burn for at least 2 hours.

Soak some fragrant wood, mesquite chips or apple-wood chips, in water for ½ hour. Wrap chips in aluminum foil and place parcel over fire or charcoal on one side of grill, leaving the other side empty. Place trout on high shelf or on part of grill bottom that is not over flame. Cover grill, and let smoke 2 to 3 hours.

Note: The trout will absorb the odor of the soaked wood. How strongly it tastes depends on the length of the smoking time and on the type of wood used. Mesquite is very popular these days, and it lends a fragrant touch to trout. In the East, however, it is expensive. Apple or cherry birch bark are both excellent for smoking.

Mary Anne's Blue Trout

YIELDS 1.38 GRAMS OF OMEGA-3 PER SERVING

Mary Anne is a friend who lives in Greenwood Lake, New York. "I don't cook a great deal of fish," she told me, "but I do make trout, blue trout, the way they make it in Germany."

The "blue" color of the trout is caused by the chemical reaction of the vinegar and the natural sticky substance on the surface of the trout's skin.

4 brook or rainbow trout	*2 parsnips, peeled and cut into*
1 cup vinegar	*strips*
1 large onion, sliced thin	*2 carrots, peeled and cut into*
1 small bunch fresh dill, cut up	*strips*
1 large piece celery root	

Tie nose of each trout to its tail, and stand them all up in the bottom of a large pot.

Heat vinegar, and pour it over each fish. Add sliced onions, cut dill, celery root, parsnips and carrots to pot. Cover and steam for 5 minutes.

Makes 4 servings.

Baked, Stuffed Trout

YIELDS 1.47 GRAMS OF OMEGA-3 PER SERVING

Boned trout are often available; stuffed, they make a striking dish. I like to serve them with boiled potatoes and steamed string beans with a vinaigrette sauce.

4 boned trout, heads on
1 10-oz. package of frozen, chopped spinach
1 onion, chopped
½ tablespoon walnut oil

¼ cup pitted prunes, chopped
1 Granny Smith apple, cored and chopped
½ cup low-fat cottage cheese

Preheat oven to 350F.

Rinse and dry trout.

Cook spinach in 2 cups of water for 5 minutes after frozen block thaws, then drain completely and press out excess water.

Sauté onion in walnut oil until soft; add prunes and apple. Cook for 3 minutes; add spinach. Add cottage cheese; mix thoroughly.

Divide stuffing into 4 parts and stuff each trout. Arrange each trout on a cookie sheet in swimming position, stuffing-side down. It won't be necessary to sew or skewer opening. The trout's weight will hold stuffing in place.

Bake for 25 minutes.

Makes 4 servings.

Mustard-And-Mushroom Stuffed Trout

YIELDS 1.38 GRAMS OF OMEGA-3 PER SERVING

Mustard is one of the spices that goes particularly well with fish. A special mustard that comes from Meaux, a city northeast of Paris, is made of whole mustard seeds as well as crushed ones. The Pommery family manufactures it using a "secret recipe." The mustard is delicious, and it does wonders for a boned trout.

4 trout, boned, washed and dried
½ cup Pommery mustard
1 dozen shallots, peeled and
    chopped
2 teaspoons tarragon, chopped (If
    you can't get fresh tarragon,
    dried will do.)
1 dozen medium-sized
    mushrooms (If possible, use
    porcini, chanterelles or oyster
    mushrooms, which are on
    sale nowadays in most
    markets. If not, the old-
    fashioned kind will do.)

2 tablespoons capers, drained
3 cloves garlic, minced
2 lemons, cut into wedges

Preheat oven to 350F. Smear inside of trout generously with mustard.

In a small bowl, combine shallots, tarragon, mushrooms, capers and garlic. Mix well.

Divide filling in 4 parts, and stuff each trout. Place each trout in swimming position on a lightly oiled baking dish; bake for 20 to 25 minutes.

Serve with lemon wedges.

Makes 4 servings.

Poached Trout In Wine

YIELDS 1.38 GRAMS OF OMEGA-3 PER SERVING

Trout poached entirely in white wine is very elegant. On the practical side, be sure to use an inexpensive wine, although never a "cooking" wine. Excellent French wines can be picked up for a few dollars a bottle.

4 trout, bones in	**3 tablespoons white horseradish**
1 bottle dry, white wine	**1 cup non-fat yogurt**
2 tablespoons minced, fresh dill	

Place trout in a large pot with a cover.

In another pot, bring wine to a boil, then pour over trout. Bring wine back to a boil again, then turn off heat and cover pan. Trout will cook in hot wine. Let stand for 15 minutes, then remove to a serving plate.

Make a sauce by combining dill, horseradish and yogurt. Whisk briskly.

Remove skin from trout and separate each cooked fillet from bone. Serve with sauce on side. Cold sauce goes well with hot, cooked trout.

Makes 4 servings.

Pan-Fried Trout

YIELDS 1.38 GRAMS OF OMEGA-3 PER SERVING

Many years ago, in the first year of my marriage, my wife and I went camping up in the Catskills. We spent the night in a mountain gorge near the banks of a rushing creek. In the morning, I made a rough oven out of mud and stones and lit a fire in it. I made dough out of flour, baking powder, salt and water, and rolled it into long strips. These I wrapped around birch sticks and left them to bake in the oven while my wife and I searched the deep pools for trout.

I caught two, no great feat if you drive them into shallow water and grab them. Sportsmen look askance at this fishing method. I gutted the trout and pan-fried them over the fire, greasing the pan lightly and using absolutely no seasoning—and they were delicious. Barbara and I still remember that breakfast of trout, coffee and baked strips of bread flavored with birch.

Trout

Of course, trout taste best in the early morning beside a rushing mountain brook with bread baked in a mud oven, but pan-fried trout are not half bad in the comfort of your own home with rolls and coffee.

The simplest method for pan-frying trout is still the best:

1 trout per person, cleaned, gutted, with bones in

1 teaspoon flour per trout
1 teaspoon oil per trout

Dust trout lightly with flour.

Grease pan with 1 teaspoon oil per trout. Fry about 4 minutes to a side over high heat, shaking pan from time to time to keep trout from sticking.

Makes 1 serving.

★ 18 ★

Anchovies, Herring And Sardines

The anchovy, a small, European fish used mainly for flavoring foods, ironically has a very high omega-3 content. It is unlikely that anyone could eat ¼ lb. of anchovies, so it cannot be considered a *basic* source of omega-3. But anchovies add flourish to **an antipasto**, and they enliven sauces with their piquancy.

Anchovies, processed herrings and tinned sardines all have some degree of salt added. People with normal blood pressure should not be concerned about eating these products occasionally. However, those with high blood pressure should be cautious about how much of these products they eat.

Sweet Pepper And Anchovy Antipasto
YIELDS .20 GRAMS OF OMEGA-3 PER SERVING

This makes great antipasto, especially for a pasta meal.

3 large, sweet red bell peppers
1 2-oz. can flat anchovy fillets in olive oil
2 tablespoons drained capers

2 cloves garlic put through a press
3 tablespoons olive oil
1 tablespoon low-acidity vinegar

Over an open gas flame, roast peppers on end of fork until completely blackened. Run cold water over them and rub off blackened skin. A stiff vegetable brush helps.

Cut top and bottom off peppers and rinse insides with water to remove seeds. Open into a long strip and cut into pieces about ¼ inch wide by 2 inches long, depending on length of pepper.

In a bowl, combine peppers, anchovies and capers.

Make dressing by adding pressed garlic to olive oil and vinegar, and whisk until semi-gelled. Pour dressing over anchovies and capers, and marinate in refrigerator for at least 8 hours, but preferably overnight.

To serve, arrange pepper strips in a circle on a serving plate, pointing each strip toward center like spokes of a wagon wheel. Put anchovies between peppers, and mound capers in the center. Dribble remaining sauce over plate.

Makes 4 servings.

Note: If you prefer not to use pressed garlic, cut cloves lengthwise and marinate them in dressing, but remove them before serving.

Anchovy Canapés

YIELDS .13–.20 GRAMS OF OMEGA-3 PER SERVING

These salty canapés go well with wine or pre-dinner drinks. Those on a salt-free diet should not eat too many.

1 can flat anchovy fillets	**¼ cup soft tofu**
½ cup low-fat cottage cheese	**1 teaspoon curry powder**
2 tablespoons non-fat yogurt	

Blend everything together in blender or food processor until smooth.

Serve on bland water biscuits or melba toast.

Makes 4 to 6 servings

Anchovied Onions

YIELDS .20 GRAMS OF OMEGA-3 PER SERVING

What do you do with leftover fish? It can be made into a salad, a casserole, a loaf or croquettes. I always keep a jar of anchovied onions in the refrigerator to serve as a side dish with cold leftover fish.

1 2-oz. tin flat anchovy fillets	1 cup olive oil
1 clove garlic put through a	¼ cup low-acidity, white vinegar
garlic press	2 large, sweet Spanish onions,
1 tablespoon capers	thinly sliced
1 tablespoon parsley	1 tablespoon whole, black
½ teaspoon oregano	peppercorns

Drain anchovy fillets. Place them in food processor with pressed garlic, capers, parsley, oregano, olive oil and vinegar. Process with a steel blade until smooth.

Place onion and peppercorns in a container and pour anchovy marinade over them to cover. Marinate for at least 24 hours—the longer, the better. If there is extra marinade, add more onion until all of marinade is used.

Makes 4 servings.

HERRING

When I was boy, my father used to take me to the Lower East Side of Manhattan to shop for delicacies. The long trip, twice a month, was always worth it. I remember his delight at selecting a fine matjes (lean) or schmaltz (fat) herring out of the huge barrels in front of the appetizer store.

Today, matjes and schmaltz herring are hard to get. One more often finds herring pickled in cream sauce or wine.

Although herring is one of the most plentiful catches in the fish industry, very few of them go to the market fresh. Most of the catch is pickled, smoked or preserved in brine. Fresh herring is a very tasty fish. The larger sizes are usually unavailable, but smaller herring under 1 lb. can be found through diligent searching.

Marinated and pickled herring can be bought at any good delicatessen, and, except for kippered herring, needn't be cooked at all. They make excellent appetizers or hors d'oeuvres. They come in fillets and can be cut into chunks and arranged on platters with toothpicks or on crackers. The pickled variety is usually sold with pickled onions, and the onions and herring make a perfect combination. The marinated variety is usually in wine and has a stronger taste than the pickled kind. For health reasons, I stay clear of herring in cream sauce, delicious though they are. If you must, eat them sparingly.

Pickled and marinated herring are often preferred because they are free of the tiny bones that you find in fresh herring. When a whole fish is split down the back for processing, the backbone is removed, and most of the little bones come out with it.

Broiled Herring

YIELDS .98–1.95 GRAMS OF OMEGA-3 PER SERVING

Whole herring should be used for broiling. Herring is too small to broil filleted without drying it out completely.

1 or 2 small herring per serving
1 teaspoon oil per herring
1 teaspoon fresh, chopped dill per herring

1 lemon, 2 wedges per herring

Oil whole fish, then broil for 3 minutes on each side, 2 inches from flame or electric coil.

Sprinkle each fish with dill and serve with lemon wedges.

Makes 1 serving.

Baked Herring

YIELDS 1.95 GRAMS OF OMEGA-3 PER SERVING

2 small herring per serving, boned and cleaned
1 small onion per herring, thinly sliced

1 tablespoon olive oil per herring
1 tablespoon no-cholesterol mayonnaise per herring
Paprika to taste

Preheat oven to 400F. Arrange herring, side by side, in a baking dish.

Sauté onion slices in olive oil.

Spread mayonnaise over herring; top with cooked onion. Sprinkle with paprika and bake for 20 minutes.

Makes 1 serving.

Note: Serve with boiled potatoes and a green vegetable.

Fried Fresh Herring

YIELDS 1.95–2.59 GRAMS OF OMEGA-3 PER SERVING

This is a Scottish dish, and of course, coming from Scotland, makes use of oatmeal.

2 herring per serving, without head, tail, or fins
⅛ cup skim milk per herring
2 tablespoons oatmeal per fish (medium-ground Scottish oatmeal is best)

1 tablespoon olive oil per herring

Let herring marinate in skim milk for ½ hour. Without drying, roll each herring on a flat plate spread evenly with oatmeal until coated.

Heat olive oil in a non-stick skillet. Fry herring 3 to 4 minutes on each side. The oatmeal crust should be nicely browned.

Note: These are delicious served with Pommery mustard.

KIPPERS

"Kippered" is synonymous with "smoked," but has come to be associated almost exclusively with herring. Grilled or baked, kippers make a delicious dish for brunch. They are a fine accompaniment to scrambled eggs. If possible do not use canned kippers; they're simply too wet. Buy dried kippers, and soak them for several hours in running cold water; or soak them in a bowl of cold water that is changed several times to remove salt. Once hydrated, they can be broiled, fried or baked.

Bloaters are herring that are allowed to get too large and fat, and then kippered. I prefer the smaller kippers, but if you have bloaters, they can be treated the same way; just give them a longer time to bake.

Baked Kippers

YIELDS .98–1.30 GRAMS OF OMEGA-3 PER SERVING

4 kippers   *¼ cup chopped, fresh parsley*
4 teaspoons olive oil per kipper   *2 lemons cut into wedges*

Preheat oven to 350F. Oil fish.
Bake for 10 minutes.
Sprinkle with parsley and garnish with lemon wedges. Serve.
Makes 4 servings.

SARDINES

The sardine is a fish without class. Most canned varieties leave much to be desired as far as taste goes. To my palate, however, some Norwegian brands have elegance and a delicate flavor.

In France, the lowly sardine has achieved greatness. A serving of sardines in the olive oil in which they have been canned can compete with any paté as an appetizer. In American supermarkets, the French brands, if you can find them, usually cost six times more than any other.

The perfect sardine is a matter of individual preference, but there are certain guidelines to follow in buying them. Tinned sardines should be small, about 3 or 4 inches in length, and headless, but with the bones in and skin on. Boneless sardines, I believe, are a waste of perfectly good and nutritious calcium.

The oil in which the sardines are packed can range from menhaden oil (a herring oil), which is nutritious although not very palatable, to olive oil, which is healthy and very tasty. The sardines should be tightly and evenly packed and allowed to ripen in the can for at least 12 months. They can be steamed, smoked or grilled.

A sardine is really a very young herring, ideally a pilchard, but sometimes a brisling or sprat. Its omega-3 content is very high. In the following recipes I have invented some unusual dishes that are based on the cuisine of different nations. I have adapted them to the reduced health-risk diet that this book promotes.

Alava Sardines

YIELDS 1.36 GRAMS OF OMEGA-3 PER SERVING

This is an adaptation of a favorite Basque dish. It can be topped with grated parmesan cheese if you have a little leeway with your cholesterol intake.

3 tablespoons olive oil
1 large, sweet Spanish onion, chopped
1 medium carrot, peeled and chopped
2 cloves garlic, minced
6 large mushrooms, chopped
1 sweet red pepper, cored, seeded and chopped

½ teaspoon ground cumin seed
4 ripe tomatoes, peeled, seeded and chopped
¼ cup very small, pitted black olives
3 3¾ oz. tins sardines, drained

In a large, non-stick frying pan, stir-fry onion, carrot and garlic in oil for 3 minutes.

Add mushrooms, pepper and ground cumin, and stir-fry 5 minutes more.

Add chopped tomatoes and pitted black olives, and cook for another 5 minutes.

Spread this mixture evenly over bottom of a shallow baking dish and arrange sardines in a layer on top of mixture. Brown it under broiler and serve hot on a bed of rice or couscous.

Makes 4 servings.

Sardine Paté

YIELDS .90 GRAMS OF OMEGA-3 PER SERVING

This is nice to set out with drinks or as an appetizer to a light summer meal.

1 packet unflavored gelatin
    (about ¼ oz.)
½ cup low-fat cottage cheese
½ cup soft tofu
3 tablespoons lemon juice
2 3¾ oz. tins sardines (boneless,
    skinless type are best for
    this)

3 scallions finely minced
1 stalk celery, finely minced
¼ cup black olives, minced
⅛ teaspoon ground fennel

Soften gelatin in ¼ cup cold water, then heat very gently until thoroughly dissolved. Let cool.

In a food processor fitted with a steel blade, process cottage cheese, tofu and lemon juice until smooth.

Add sardines, a few at a time, and continue processing. When all sardines have been added, transfer mixture to a bowl, scraping down sides of processor with a spatula.

Fold scallions, celery, olives, fennel and softened gelatin into sardine mixture. Mix thoroughly and pack into either a mold or serving bowl. Chill at least 6 hours, but preferably overnight.

Makes 4 servings.

Norwegian Sardine Spread

YIELDS .45 GRAMS OF OMEGA-3 PER SERVING

This is a fine spread for parties or to go with wine before dinner. I like it with water biscuits and a dish of tiny pickled onions. Put some spread on a cracker, and top it with an onion. Try it with martinis.

1 cup low-fat cottage cheese	¼ teaspoon paprika
3 tablespoons lemon juice	
1 3¾ oz. tin Norwegian smoked sardines, with bones and skin	

In a food processor or blender, mix cottage cheese with lemon juice until there are no lumps.

Add sardines, a few at a time, and blend thoroughly.

Add paprika and blend again.

Serve in a small bowl with biscuits or strips of toasted white bread. Or pour into a mold and chill. Present on a bed of lettuce. It's good either way.

Makes 4 servings.

Baked Sardines

YIELDS 1.70 GRAMS OF OMEGA-3 PER SERVING

Tinned sardines baked in a tomato and wine sauce are superb.

1 tablespoon olive oil	2 tomatoes, peeled, seeded and chopped
6 scallions, chopped in small rings	¼ teaspoon turmeric
2 cloves garlic, put through a press	½ teaspoon rosemary
1 cup dry, light red wine	4 3¾ oz. tins smoked sardines

Preheat oven to 350F.

In a non-stick pan or wok, stir-fry scallions and garlic in oil 5 minutes.

Add wine, tomatoes, turmeric and rosemary, and simmer for about 20 minutes.

Place ½ sardines in a shallow baking dish and pour sauce over them. Place rest of sardines on top of sauce and bake in oven for 5 minutes.

Serve over rice.

Makes 4 servings as a main dish.

❧ *19* ❧

Luxury Fish And Unusual Vegetables

These recipes are made from fish you have to search for. Both in terms of health benefits and taste, they're worth it, although sometimes prohibitively expensive. As a special bonus, I offer two recipes made from common but unusual vegetables that are exceptionally high in omega-3.

If you have been patronizing a store for some time, you can ask the retailer to pick up a particular type of fish when he buys his supplies at the wholesale market. Most will be willing to oblige a good customer. Others will be glad to tell you when they expect to obtain a particular type of fish and when it is in season or available.

Lake trout, as opposed to its cousins in rivers and streams, has very high omega-3 content. But a trout is a trout, and lake trout, though scarcer than speckled, rainbow, brook trout or arctic char, is equally as delicious—some people say it is even more so. It can be cooked by any of the methods described in the section under trout, or it can be baked or broiled as in the recipes below.

Lake trout varies in size from three pounds to 15 pounds, depending on the age of the fish. Interestingly enough, larger trout are far more tasty.

If there is a fisherman in your family and a cold-water lake within striking distance, let him or her try trolling for lake trout in late September. It will be well worth it.

Broiled Lake Trout

YIELDS 4.6 GRAMS OF OMEGA-3 PER SERVING

I've put this recipe outside the regular trout section because lake trout is not only scarcer than its river cousins, but much higher in omega-3.

4 medium-sized trout fillets, with
    skin left on
1 teaspoon olive oil
2 tablespoons fresh parsley,
    minced

¼ cup dry, white wine
⅛–¼ teaspoon freshly ground
    black pepper
2 tablespoons non-fat yogurt
1 lemon, cut into wedges

Arrange fillets in a well-oiled broiling pan, skin- side down.

Blend oil, parsley, wine and pepper with a whisk and pour over fillets.

Broil fillets 2 inches from flame for 5 to 7 minutes.

Remove fillets to warm serving platter. Add yogurt to drippings in pan and blend until smooth. Pour over fish. Serve with wedges of lemon.

Makes 4 servings.

Baked Lake Trout

YIELDS 4.6 GRAMS OF OMEGA-3 PER SERVING

Lake trout, especially the larger ones, are perfect for baking. Lake trout bakes best with the head on, but if you prefer, cut off head before stuffing or just before serving.

1 small head celery
1 tablespoon olive oil
2 large onions, chopped
1 cup unflavored bread crumbs
¼ teaspoon savory
¼ teaspoon pepper

1 lake trout, about 6 lbs., cleaned
2 medium carrots, thinly sliced
1 teaspoon dried marjoram
2 cups dry, white wine
1 lemon, sliced very thin

Preheat oven to 400F.

Prepare stuffing by chopping all but 2 stalks of celery. Heat olive oil in large, non-stick fry pan. Sauté celery and onions for 5 minutes. Add bread crumbs, savory and pepper. If stuffing is too stiff, gradually add a few tablespoons of hot water.

Stuff trout and close with small skewer.

Chop 2 remaining stalks of celery. In a baking dish large enough to hold fish, make a bed of celery and carrots. Sprinkle with marjoram. Place stuffed fish on vegetables and pour wine over fish.

Bake for 30 minutes, basting every 10 minutes with wine sauce.

Serve by removing baked fish to a warm platter. Remove skewer and skin; pour wine sauce over fish. Decorate with lemon slices.

Note: I also like to remove stuffing and to bone fish before pouring sauce.

Makes 6 servings.

SPINY DOGFISH

The spiny dogfish, high in omega-3 content, is really a shark that is about three or four feet long when fully grown. It is rarely found in fish markets. The shark commonly sold is the mako, a mackerel shark which, although very tasty, is much lower in omega-3. It has only .5 grams in every 100 grams of fish. Incidentally, the mako shark has, in some unscrupulous restaurants, been substituted for swordfish; they have a similar flavor. The swordfish is another very tasty fish, but also extremely low in omega-3: only .2 grams per 100 grams of fish.

Chinese Walnut Dogfish

YIELDS 2.3 TO 2.6 GRAMS OF OMEGA-3 PER SERVING

If you are fortunate enough to get some spiny dogfish, this recipe, based on a Chinese dish, is a good one. The same recipe can be used with fresh herring, bluefish or mullet.

1 heaping teaspoon cornstarch	1 cup sliced bamboo shoots
¼ cup dry sherry	½ cup sliced water chestnuts
1 tablespoon walnut oil (or olive oil)	1 cup spinach leaves, cut into strips
1 lb. dogfish cut in bite-sized pieces	½ cup walnuts, chopped coarsely
2 scallions, chopped	1 tablespoon light soy sauce

Dissolve cornstarch in sherry.

Heat oil in a wok and cook fish for 5 minutes. (A large frying pan can be substituted for a wok.) Lift out with a slotted spoon.

Add scallions, bamboo shoots, water chestnuts and spinach leaves to oil remaining in wok and stir-fry for 2 minutes.

Return fish to wok and add walnuts.

Mix soy sauce with sherry and dissolved cornstarch, and add it to wok. Stir-fry until sauce thickens.

Serve over rice.

Makes 4 servings.

SABLEFISH

The sablefish is a delicious West Coast fish high in omega-3. It is very rare east of the Rockies, except in its exquisite smoked form. No Sunday brunch in Manhattan is complete without a slab of smoked sablefish to complement bagels, lox and cream cheese. But if you're lucky enough to get fresh sablefish, try it broiled.

Broiled Sablefish

YIELDS 3.45 GRAMS OF OMEGA-3 PER SERVING

The paprika in the oil in this recipe will give white sablefish a pleasant, browned appearance once cooked.

¼ *teaspoon paprika*	*Sablefish steaks, enough for 4*
1 tablespoon olive oil	*portions*

Preheat broiler. Whisk paprika into olive oil and spread it over bottom of broiling pan. Put steaks on oiled pan, then turn steaks so that oiled side is up. One tablespoon oil will suffice for 4 steaks because the gelatinous flesh of sablefish prevents it from drying out.

Broil 3 inches below flame or electric coil. For a 1-inch thick steak, broil 5 minutes on each side.

Makes 4 servings.

Baked Sablefish

YIELDS 2.31 TO 3.45 GRAMS OF OMEGA-3 PER SERVING

Although sablefish can be baked plain with only a bit of oil rubbed on the skin, the version presented here is delicious and festive. If you choose the more spartan baking method, allow 7 minutes to the lb.

You can also bake or broil smoked sablefish, but this is a bit like gilding the lily. Smoked sable is perfect uncooked, thinly sliced and served with capers, heavy rye bread and paper-thin slices of sweet onion.

1 4-lb. sablefish, cleaned and gutted	4 stalks celery, chopped
2 tablespoons olive oil	2 cloves garlic, minced
1 cup dry, red wine	2 ripe tomatoes, peeled, seeded, chopped
2 medium onions, chopped	½ cup chopped, fresh parsley

Preheat oven to 400F.

Oil fish with 1 tablespoon olive oil and place in a suitably sized baking pan. Pour red wine around it and bake. Allow 7 minutes to a lb., or approximately 30 minutes.

While fish bakes, sauté onions, celery and garlic in remaining olive oil until soft. Add tomatoes and simmer over low heat for 20 minutes.

Remove fish from baking pan, reserving liquids. Remove skin and fillet fish. Add pan liquids to vegetables along with parsley. Stir well. Place fillets on serving plate and pour sauce around them.

Makes 4 to 6 servings.

STURGEON

Sturgeon feed on shellfish in the open sea, and like salmon they move upstream in the spring to deposit their eggs on the riverbed—a perfect waste of good caviar! Unhappily, sturgeon has become so rare that it is almost never available, and its even-rarer caviar is priced out of the reach of most people.

The sturgeon that *is* caught is usually saved for smoking. Smoked sturgeon is heavenly, far surpassing smoked sablefish. As great as its taste is, and though rich in omega-3, its prohibitive price does not make it worth considering as a regular source of omega-3 for the average person.

In modest amounts, smoked sturgeon can be a delightful addition to a brunch. I usually serve it on a platter with smoked whitefish, Nova Scotia smoked salmon and sable. Sweet onions, marinated in low-acidity vinegar and sliced paper-thin, makes a good accompaniment, along with capers, cream cheese, low-calorie crisp breads and warm bagels.

LAKE WHITEFISH

The north central part of the United States is particularly familiar with lake whitefish, an extremely important freshwater fish, rich in omega-3. I remember my surprise and delight on first tasting smoked lake whitefish on a visit to Minneapolis. A city boy, I had assumed that smoked whitefish was a product of New York City delicatessens. Fortunately, it can be found throughout almost the entire country.

Stuffed Whitefish

YIELDS 3.45 GRAMS OF OMEGA-3 PER SERVING

4 ½-lb. skinless whitefish fillets
4 tablespoons lemon juice
1 tablespoon olive oil
Ground black pepper to taste
1 large onion, finely chopped
½ cup bread crumbs
¼ cup tofu

¼ cup low-fat cottage cheese
½ teaspoon tarragon
2 egg whites or 1 teaspoon egg
*   substitute*
½ lb. mushrooms, sliced
1 cup dry, white wine

Preheat oven to 375F. Wash and dry fillets and brush each with lemon juice. Oil a baking pan with olive oil and lay fillets out on it. Add pepper to taste.

In a bowl, mix chopped onion, bread crumbs, tofu, cottage cheese and tarragon thoroughly. Add egg whites or egg substitute and mushrooms, and gradually add white wine in order to just bind stuffing.

Put stuffing in the center of each fillet and pull ends over stuffing.

Then roll fillets over so that ends are down. The weight of fillet and stuffing will hold the ends in. No skewers are necessary.

Pour remaining wine around fillets. Bake for 30 minutes.

Makes 4 servings.

Baked Whole Lake Whitefish

YIELDS 3.45 GRAMS OF OMEGA-3 PER SERVING

The whole whitefish can be baked without stuffing. Skinned and boned it goes nicely with any well-flavored sauce.

1 4–5-lb. whitefish, head on or off	*2 large carrots, shredded*
	1 teaspoon dried tarragon
1 tablespoon olive oil	*1 cup dry, white wine*
2 large onions, sliced	

Preheat oven to 400F.

Rub fish with olive oil.

In a baking pan large enough for fish, make a bed of onions and shredded carrots and sprinkle tarragon over it. Lay fish on bed and douse with wine.

Bake for 30 minutes or until fish flakes easily with a fork. Baste with pan juices every 10 minutes.

When done, remove fish to a warm serving platter and empty pan juices into a blender or food processor. Blend thoroughly and serve in a gravy boat with fish.

Makes 4 to 6 servings depending on size of fish.

MULLET

Mullet is not well-known in the northern part of the United States, but it is a staple in the South. The Egyptians cultivated the mullet in ancient times, raising it in the delta of the Nile. The Romans cultivated it in pools, and today the Chinese cultivate gray mullet in brackish ponds and freshwater mullet further inland.

Mullet is available in most fish markets, and the fillets can be broiled, stuffed or baked. Because it is a small fish, usually the entire fish is broiled or baked.

Baked Whole Mullet

YIELDS 2.53 GRAMS OF OMEGA-3 PER SERVING

I like to think that the buttermilk and cornflakes gives this dish a Southern accent.

4 small mullet, dressed　　　*½ cup bread crumbs*
1 cup buttermilk　　　*1 tablespoon polyunsaturated oil*
½ cup cornflakes　　　*1 lemon, cut into wedges*

Soak dressed fish in buttermilk for at least 1 hour, longer if practical.

Preheat oven to 450F. Combine cornflakes and bread crumbs in a plastic bag, and roll them with a rolling pin or bottle until cornflakes are crumbled.

Put wet mullet in plastic or small paper bag and shake until completely covered with bread crumb-cornflake mixture. I have found this to be the tidiest way of coating fish. They can be coated in a plate filled with coating mixture, but the shake-bag method is more efficient.

Oil a baking dish large enough to hold fish and lay fish in it. Bake for 15 minutes. Serve with lemon wedges. At 1 fish per serving, this makes 4 servings. A 2-lb. fish should yield about ½ lb. of edible meat.

TWO UNUSUAL VEGETABLES

Here are two unusual vegetables. With a little ingenuity, and some foraging in the outdoors or in local greengrocer markets, you should be able to find them.

Pickled Purslane

Purslane, a common garden weed, is a bountiful source of omega-3. It is also tasty green, raw, cooked, frozen or pickled. In his book, Stalking the Wild Asparagus, *the late Euell Gibbons suggests that the entire plant, leaf, stem and flowerbud can be eaten. But the very best parts are the pinched-off, tender leaf tips.*

The tips can be washed and boiled for 10 minutes, or eaten raw in salad. The plant is very oily, oozing with omega-3. Its mucilaginous character makes it a great thickener for soups and stews. The fat, tender stems of the purslane can be pickled easily. This goes well with any broiled fish.

1 cup distilled white vinegar
2 cups cold water
¼ cup salt
½ teaspoon alum
2 dill flowers

2 garlic cloves
2 small red hot peppers
*Enough clean purslane to loosely
   pack 2 2-pint jars*
2 2-pint pickling jars, with tops

Mix pickling fluid by combining vinegar, water, salt and alum.

Put 1 dill flower, 1 garlic clove and 1 pepper in the bottom of each jar. Pack jar loosely with purslane stems. Pour in pickling fluid to cover.

Store in a cool, dark place for at least 1 month.

Broccoli Di Rape

This green, high in omega-3, is available in most supermarkets and produce stores in late winter and spring and in some areas all year round. It is usually cooked with spinach. The canola oil from its seed is rich in linolenic acid.

1 lb. fresh spinach	**1 clove garlic, minced**
½ lb. broccoli di rape	**Pepper to taste**
1 small head cabbage	**Lemon wedges**
2 tablespoons olive oil	

Wash spinach and broccoli di rape, and cut off the tough stems of both.

Remove outer leaves of cabbage and discard. Cut head in quarters.

In 4 quarts boiling water, cook broccoli di rape and cabbage for 10 minutes. Remove and drain.

Put wet spinach leaves in a pot and steam 5 minutes with only the water that adheres to the leaves.

Chop cooked greens into small pieces.

Heat oil in skillet. Sauté garlic and greens for 10 minutes. Serve hot with pepper to taste and lemon wedges.

Makes 6 servings.

20

Fish And Pasta

Once I got into cooking, I began to try new dishes as I felt a growing sense of confidence, exploration and discovery. I felt proud of my accomplishments when my wife or our guests praised what I had done. Pasta was, and remains, one of my favorite dishes, especially because it required only a minimum of kitchen know-how as I learned how to cook. After all, what's there to learn about boiling water?

After I had served him linguini with pesto sauce, my son came home from school on his next visit with a pasta machine for me. One of my daughters, after tasting my pasta and seafood salad, contributed a pasta drying rack. Although I don't include recipes for fresh pasta in this book, I encourage you to learn how to make it: freshly-made pasta is divine.

Pasta is also economical, nutritious and versatile. In combination with fish, its health benefits increase dramatically. Like fish, it is a valuable source of protein (15 percent) and is low in fat (1.5 percent). As a diet food it is superb because it releases complex carbohydrates slowly and evenly without sudden surges of sugar.

It is my hope that the recipes that follow will inspire you to experiment and try different combinations of pasta shapes and different kinds of fish.

Bob's Fish And Pasta

YIELDS .84 TO 1.15 GRAMS OF OMEGA-3 PER SERVING

Bob is an accomplished artist and a very good cook. While most people bring a bottle of wine to a dinner at a friend's, Bob brings pickled mushrooms, a paté or brandied fruit. At home, Bob cooks for his two teen-age boys and claims that the only dish that fills them up, and is healthy to boot, is his linguini with salmon and scallops. Fish, he insists, goes beautifully with pasta.

1 onion, chopped
1 carrot, chopped fine
2 cloves garlic, minced
1½ cups chicken broth
½ package frozen peas
½ cup white wine

1 lb. salmon, cut into small pieces
½ lb. bay scallops
1 1-lb. package linguini
1 tablespoon olive oil
1 cup fresh parsley, chopped

Sauté onion, carrot and garlic in ¼ cup chicken broth. Keep adding chicken broth as vegetables absorb it. Sauté for 5 minutes or more until onion is soft. You may use about ¾ of broth.

Add frozen peas, wine and rest of broth. Simmer 2 minutes, then add salmon and scallops. Cook 5 minutes on low heat.

Remove from heat. Cook linguini *al dente* according to package directions. Drain and toss with olive oil in a warmed serving bowl.

Add salmon and scallop sauce to linguini; toss and serve.

Makes 6 servings.

Lasagna Di Mare

YIELDS .51 TO .76 GRAMS OF OMEGA-3 PER SERVING

This mix of fish and pasta is a rather unusual seafood lasagna. It's a dish that requires a bit of work, but it is well worth it. We made it for guests recently, one of whom had just recovered from a quadruple bypass operation and was very concerned about cholesterol. I assured him it had almost none, but did have some healthy omega-3.

This lasagna can be assembled beforehand and then baked 1 hour before serving. That allows you to get out of the kitchen and sit down with guests before eating. When I have guests I want to spend time with them, not in the kitchen! A green salad and a loaf of Italian bread go well with this dish.

Sauce

1 large onion, chopped
4 cloves garlic, chopped
3 tablespoons olive oil
1 1 lb. 12 oz.-can tomato purée
2 tablespoons basil purée or pesto
    (see below)

½ cup dry, white wine
2 teaspoons powdered fennel seed
Pepper to taste

1 1-lb. package lasagna

Filling:

2 lbs. mussels, bearded, washed
    well
3 tablespoons basil purée (see
    below)
16 oz. low-fat cottage cheese
1 cup soft tofu, rinsed and
    drained
4 egg whites or 2 teaspoons egg
    replacer

1 10-oz. package frozen spinach
1 lb. imitation crabmeat,
    shredded
1 sweet red pepper, cored and
    diced
8 small scallions, chopped
2 tablespoons Pernod
1 lb. bay scallops

In a large pot, sauté onion and garlic in 1 tablespoon olive oil until onion is translucent.

Add tomato purée to garlic and onion. Add 2 tablespoons basil purée, wine, powdered fennel and pepper to taste. Simmer for 45 minutes on very low heat, stirring occasionally.

While sauce is cooking, prepare noodles. Bring large pot of cold water to boil. Add noodles, 1 or 2 at a time. Cook noodles until slightly firmer than *al dente*. Remove from heat and carefully arrange on a towel or in cold water, until needed.

Put 1 cup water in a large pot and add mussels. Steam mussels for 5 minutes or until opened. Shell and put aside, discarding those that have not opened.

Prepare filling. Process cottage cheese, tofu and egg whites (or egg substitute) in a food processor fitted with a steel blade until smooth.

Cook chopped spinach according to package directions and drain.

Add all but ½ cup of spinach to cottage cheese mixture and set aside. Mix in crabmeat, chopped red pepper, scallions and 3 tablespoons basil purée.

When sauce is cooked, add 2 tablespoons Pernod; stir and set aside approximately ¼ cup. Add steamed mussels and scallops to remaining sauce and remove from heat at once.

To assemble lasagna, use a flat, 2-quart lasagna dish or baking pan. Spread and spread ¼ cup sauce over bottom. Arrange a layer of noodles over sauce, then arrange ½ of cottage cheese over noodles, spreading it out evenly. Pour ½ of seafood sauce over cheese layer. Arrange another layer of noodles over sauce and remaining ½ cup spinach over noodles and cover with remaining cheese. Arrange noodles on top to create final layer and cover with remaining sauce. Lasagna can now be refrigerated for up to 8 hours.

Preheat oven to 350F. If refrigerated, allow lasagna to come to room temperature. Bake for 30 minutes, until brown and bubbling.

Let cool at room temperature for 15 minutes. Cut into squares and serve.

Makes 4 to 6 servings.

Note: A new brand of packaged mussels from Maine are particularly clean and pollution-free and available at most big supermarkets.

Basil Purée (Pesto)

The classic Italian pesto, although included in the variations, uses cheese that is very salty. Thus I prefer the plainer version for health reasons.

2 cups basil leaves, without stems   6 tablespoons olive oil

Place basil leaves in blender container and blend for 2 seconds. Add oil 1 tablespoon at a time until all oil is blended in. Set aside.Combine basil leaves and olive oil in a blender, and blend well. Set aside.

Variation 1: Add 3 tablespoons freshly grated parmesan cheese.
Variation 2: Add 2 cloves crushed garlic after adding cheese.
Variation 3: Add 3 tablespoons pignoli (pine nuts).
Variation 4: Use fresh spinach leaves without stems instead of basil.

Pasta-Surf Salad

YIELDS 1.27 GRAMS OF OMEGA-3 PER SERVING

This is a quick dish for those summer nights when you haven't the energy to spend too much time cooking. All it requires is slicing, chopping and poaching.

Dressing

1 tablespoon Dijon mustard
3 tablespoons low-acidity vinegar
½ teaspoon tarragon, fresh or
   dried, finely chopped

¼ cup walnut oil

Whisk mustard into vinegar; it will not blend well with walnut oil unless mixed with vinegar first.
Add tarragon and oil and whisk together until smooth. Set aside.

Salad

½ lb. small elbow macaroni
¼ lb. bay scallops
½ lb. small shrimp, shelled and
   deveined
½ lb. imitation crab meat,
   shredded
1 sweet red bell pepper, seeded
   and chopped

1 sweet yellow bell pepper, seeded
   and chopped
3 scallions, chopped
10 leaves fresh spinach, stems
   removed, washed and torn
   into small pieces
1 cup small, black olives, pitted

Prepare macaroni according to package directions; drain and cool.
Place scallops and shrimp in large pot of boiling water. Lower heat and poach for 5 minutes. Drain and let cool in large bowl. Add to imitation crabmeat.
Add peppers, scallions, spinach leaves, black olives, and cooled macaroni.
Add dressing and toss gently.
Makes 6 servings.

Fabulous Fusilli

YIELDS .88 TO 1.78 GRAMS OF OMEGA-3 PER SERVING

This pasta dish is a bit of trouble, but well worth the effort. The last time I served it, my guests labeled it "fabulous," and I've decided to call it that. It will serve from 4 to 6 people, depending on their appetites.

2 lbs. mussels, bearded and
    thoroughly rinsed
½ lb. fresh salmon, either fillets
    or boned steaks
1 10-oz. package frozen peas
½ cup olive oil
Juice of 2 lemons
3 scallions, finely chopped
1 large tomato, peeled, seeded
    and diced

2 dill sprigs, chopped, or 4
    teaspoons dill weed
1 teaspoon ground pepper
½ lb. Nova Scotia smoked
    salmon
1 1-lb. package fusilli

Preheat broiler. Rinse mussels in cold water, at least 3 rinses. Bring 1 cup of water to a boil in a pot with a cover. Add mussels. Steam for 5 minutes until all are opened. Discard any mussels that have not opened. Shell mussels and discard shells. Place mussels in large bowl.

Coat broiling pan with oil. If using a steak, turn so that both sides are oiled. If a fillet, put cut side to oil, then turn and broil with skin-side down. Broil for 4 to 5 minutes for a fillet, 4 minutes on each side for a 1-inch thick steak. Shred salmon and add to mussels.

Prepare frozen peas according to package instructions. Drain and add to salmon and mussels.

Combine olive oil, lemon juice, scallions, tomato, dill and pepper. Pour over the mussel-salmon-peas mixture.

Shred smoked salmon and add to mixture. Toss lightly. Set aside to marinate.

Bring large pot of salted water to boil. Add a tablespoon of oil to prevent water from boiling over. Add fusilli and cook until *al dente*, approximately 5 to 6 minutes. Drain.

In a large serving bowl combine marinated mussel-salmon mixture with fusilli.

Makes 4 to 6 servings.

Note: Serve with a crisp Italian bread. A salad is optional: the fusilli is a fabulous meal in itself.

Green Anchovy Pasta

YIELDS 3.16 GRAMS OF OMEGA-3 PER SERVING

This is a strong dish for those who enjoy the taste of anchovies and garlic. It's good for a very cold winter night.

½ cup walnut oil
1 tin flat anchovies
½ cup fresh sweet basil leaves
½ cup fresh parsley, chopped

4 large cloves garlic, put through
a press
1 1-lb. package linguini

Place walnut oil, anchovies, basil leaves, parsley and pressed garlic in a blender or a food processor with a steel blade. Process or blend until smooth.

Put blended sauce in a small pan over very low heat.

Cook linguini according to package instruction. Drain and transfer to serving casserole.

Pour sauce over linguini and serve.

Makes 4 servings.

Note: This recipe calls for walnut oil because the amount of omega-3 in a 2-oz. can of anchovies is minimal. The walnut oil adds enough linolenic acid to make this pasta dish heart-healthy.

Pasta With Sardine Sauce

YIELDS .67 TO 1.0 GRAMS OF OMEGA-3 PER SERVING

Sardines and raisins? You'll be delighted and surprised by the taste of this pasta dish.

3 tablespoons raisins
1 head fresh fennel
¼ cup olive oil
1 medium onion, coarsely
*   chopped*
2 3³/₄-oz. tins smoked sardines,
*   with bones and skin*

½ tin flat anchovy fillets
2 tablespoons red wine vinegar
¼ teaspoon turmeric
½ teaspoon dried sweet basil
1 lb. penne, or any short, tubular
*   pasta*
4 tablespoons pine nuts

Soak raisins in warm water.

Chop up fennel head, leaves and all, and boil in plenty of water for about 15 minutes. Remove fennel with a slotted spoon and set aside. You can leave this water at a simmer, and use it to boil pasta later.

Heat olive oil in a skillet, and sauté chopped onions until they are soft. Add sardines to oil. Chop anchovies and add them along with the red wine vinegar, turmeric and basil to oil.

Mix together, breaking up sardines, and cook at low heat for 5 minutes.

Drain raisins and add to sauce.

Chop fennel very fine and add to sauce.

Cook pasta in fennel water to degree you prefer. Drain; add sauce and pine nuts. Toss gently and serve.

Makes 4 to 6 servings.

Salmon Pasta With Grapes And Nuts

YIELDS .29 TO .48 GRAMS OF OMEGA-3 PER SERVING

I learned this recipe from a friend in California. The crunchiness of the nuts and the sweetness of the grapes are a surprising complement to the taste of the fish.

3 green onions
3 tablespoons margarine
1 clove garlic, minced
1 cup skim milk
6 oz. yogurt cheese, room
   temperature, cut into chunks
¾ teaspoon finely shredded lemon
   peel
1½–2 teaspoon lemon juice

White pepper to taste
¾ lb. fresh fettucini or 1 8- or
   10-oz. package dried
   fettucini
½ cup slivered almonds
1 cup seedless grapes, cut in half
6 oz. smoked salmon, cut into ½-
   inch squares

Slice onions, separating white portions from green tops. Reserve tops.

Melt 3 tablespoons margarine in medium saucepan. Add sliced white portions of onions and garlic. Sauté until onion is translucent.

Add skim milk and yogurt cheese. Cook over medium-low heat, stirring constantly, until cheese melts and sauce is smooth. Remove from heat.

Season with lemon peel, lemon juice and white pepper.

Bring a large kettle of water to a rapid boil. Add fresh or packaged pasta. Cook fresh pasta about 3 minutes; cook packaged pasta according to package directions, until *al dente*. Drain and return to kettle.

Add cream sauce; toss and distribute.

Reserve about ¼ cup each of slivered almonds, grapes and onion tops for garnish. Add remaining almonds, grapes, onion tops and salmon to pasta mixture.

Pour onto a platter or into a large serving bowl. Garnish with reserved almonds, onion tops and grapes.

Makes 5 to 6 servings.

Stir-Fried Salmon Over Linguini

YIELDS .56 TO .81 GRAMS OF OMEGA-3 PER SERVING

If you've planned a meal for two and suddenly another couple turns up, this recipe is a good way to stretch your ingredients and still turn out a creditable meal. The wok is a wonderful way to cook for those who must follow a restricted diet. I resisted buying an electric one for a long time, feeling that no Chinese cook would use one, but my wife won me over, and I'm glad she did. Lined with a non-stick coating, the electric wok allows you to use a minimum amount of oil in cooking, and the controlled heat is perfect for stir-frying, steaming, and, if you're so inclined, deep-frying. As in most of the recipes, salt has been left out of this one, but freshly ground pepper should be added, in quantity, at the table.

1 tablespoon polyunsaturated oil	**1 teaspoon dried oregano**
1 medium onion, thinly sliced	**1 teaspoon dried basil**
2 cloves garlic, minced	**2 tablespoons capers, drained**
½ cup small, pitted black olives	**½ lb. salmon fillet, cut into small**
1 sweet red bell pepper, sliced	**strips**
into thin strips	**1 1-lb. package linguini**

In a wok, or a large frying pan, heat oil. Add onions and garlic and sauté 2 minutes.

Add olives and red bell pepper, and stir-fry 2 minutes.

Sprinkle with oregano and basil; add capers and salmon strips. Stirring constantly to avoid burning, stir-fry over high heat for 2 minutes or until salmon turns pale pink. Remove from heat and let stand. Prepare linguini, *al dente*, in 4 quarts of boiling water or according to package directions. Drain and, in a serving casserole, add salmon and olive mixture to linguini.

Makes 4 servings.

APPENDIX

Omega-3 Fatty Acids And Other Fat Components In Selected Foods

PER 100 GRAMS EDIBLE PORTION RAW

Food item	Total fat	Total saturated	Total monoun-saturated	Total polyun-saturated	Total Omega-3	Cholesterol
Beef	g	g	g	g	g	mg
Chuck, blade roast, all grades, separable lean & fat, raw	23.6	10.0	10.8	0.9	0.3	73
Ground, regular, raw	27.0	10.8	11.6	1.0	.2	85
Round, full cut, choice grade, separable lean & fat, raw	17.5	7.4	7.8	.7	.2	66
Separable fat from retail cuts, raw	70.9	31.0	32.4	2.6	1.0	99
T-Bone steak, choice grade, lean only, raw	8.0	3.2	3.4	.3	Tr	60
T-Bone steak, choice grade, separable lean & fat, raw	26.1	11.2	11.7	1.0	.3	71
Cereal Grains	g	g	g	g	g	mg
Barley, bran	5.3	1.0	.6	2.7	.3	0
Corn, germ	30.8	3.9	7.6	18.0	.3	0

Source: United States Department of Agriculture, Human Nutrition Information Service (May, 1986)

Food item	Total fat	Total satu-rated	Total monoun-saturated	Total polyun-saturated	Total Omega-3	Cholesterol
Oats, germ	30.7	5.6	11.1	12.4	1.4	0
Rice, bran	19.2	3.6	7.3	6.6	.2	0
Wheat, bran	4.6	.7	.7	2.4	.2	0
Wheat, germ	10.9	1.9	1.6	6.6	.7	0
Wheat, hard red winter	2.5	.4	.3	1.2	.1	0
Dairy and Egg Products	g	g	g	g	g	mg
Cheese, Cheddar	33.1	21.1	9.0	.9	.4	105
Cheese, Roquefort	30.6	19.3	8.5	1.3	.7	90
Cream, heavy whipping	37.0	23.0	10.7	1.4	.5	137
Milk, whole	3.3	2.1	1.0	.1	.1	14
Egg yolk, chicken, raw	32.9	9.9	13.2	4.3	.1	1,602
Fats and Oils	g	g	g	g	g	mg
Butter	81.1	50.5	23.4	3.0	1.2	2.19
Butter oil	99.5	61.9	28.7	3.7	1.5	256
Chicken fat	99.8	29.8	44.7	20.9	1.0	85
Duck fat	99.8	33.2	49.3	12.9	1.0	100
Lard	100	39.2	45.1	11.2	1.0	95
Linseed Oil	100	9.4	20.2	66.0	53.3	0
Margarine, hard, soybean	80.5	16.7	39.3	20.9	1.5	0
Margarine, hard, soybean & soybean (hydrog.)	80.5	13.1	37.6	26.2	1.9	0
Margarine, hard, soybean (hydrog.) & palm	80.5	17.5	31.2	28.2	2.3	0
Margarine, hard, soybean (hydrog.) & cottonseed	80.5	15.6	36.1	25.3	2.8	0
Margarine, hard, soybean (hydrog.) & palm (hydrog.)	80.5	15.1	32.0	29.8	3.0	0
Margarine, liquid, soybean (hydrog.), soybean, & cottonseed	80.6	13.2	28.1	35.8	2.4	0
Margarine, soft, soybean (hydrog.) & cottonseed	80.4	16.5	31.3	29.1	1.6	0

Omega-3 Fatty Acids and Other Fat Components in Selected Fooods

Food item	Total fat	Total saturated	Total monounsaturated	Total polyunsaturated	Total Omega-3	Cholesterol
Margarine, soft, soybean (hydrog.) & palm	80.4	17.1	25.2	34.6	1.9	0
Margarine, soft, soybean, soybean (hydrog.) & cottonseed (hydrog.)	80.4	16.1	30.7	30.1	2.8	0
Mutton tallow	100	47.3	40.6	7.8	2.3	102
Rapeseed oil	100	6.8	55.5	33.3	11.1	0
Rice bran oil	100	19.7	39.3	35.0	1.6	0
Salad dressing, comm., blue cheese, reg.	52.3	9.9	12.3	27.8	3.7	17
Salad dressing, comm., Italian, reg.	48.3	7.0	11.2	28.0	3.3	0
Salad dressing, comm., mayonnaise-type	33.4	4.7	9.0	18.0	2.0	26
Salad dressing, comm., Thousand Island, reg.	35.7	6.0	8.3	19.8	2.5	0
Salad dressing, home recipe, French	70.2	12.6	20.7	33.7	1.9	0
Shortening, household, lard & veg. oil	100	40.3	44.4	10.9	1.1	56
Shortening, special-purpose, for cake mixes, soybean (hydrog.) & cottonseed (hydrog.)	100	27.2	54.2	14.1	1.1	0
Shortening, special-purpose, heavy-duty, frying, soybean (hydrog.)	100	18.4	43.7	33.5	2.4	0
Soybean lecithin	100	15.3	10.9	45.1	5.1	0
Soybean oil	100	14.4	23.3	57.9	6.8	0
Spread, margarine-like, about 60% fat, soybean (hydrog.) & palm (hydrog.)	60.8	14.1	26.0	18.1	1.6	0
Spread, margarine-like, about 60% fat, soybean (hydrog.), palm (hydrog.), & palm	60.8	13.5	24.1	20.4	1.6	0
Tomato seed oil	100	19.7	22.8	53.1	2.3	0
Walnut oil	100	9.1	22.8	63.3	10.4	0
Wheat germ oil	100	18.8	15.1	61.7	6.9	0

The OMEGA-3 Breakthrough

Food item	Total fat	Total saturated	Total monoun-saturated	Total polyun-saturated	Total Omega-3	Cholesterol
Fruits	g	g	g	g	g	mg
Avocados, California, raw	17.3	2.6	11.2	2.0	.1	0
Raspberries, raw	.6	Tr	Tr	.3	.1	0
Strawberries, raw	.4	Tr	Tr	.2	.1	0
Lamb and Veal	g	g	g	g	g	mg
Lamb, leg, raw (83% lean, 17% fat)	17.6	8.1	7.1	1.0	.3	71
Lamb, loin, raw (72% lean, 28% fat)	27.4	12.8	11.2	1.6	.5	71
Veal, leg round with rump, raw (87% lean, 13% fat)	9.0	3.8	3.7	.6	.1	71
Legumes	g	g	g	g	g	mg
Beans, common, dry	1.5	0.2	0.1	0.9	0.6	0
Chickpeas, dry	5.0	.5	1.1	2.3	.1	0
Cowpeas, dry	1.9	.6	.1	.8	.3	0
Lentils, dry	1.2	.2	.2	.5	.1	0
Lima beans, dry	1.4	.3	.1	7	.2	0
Peas, garden, dry	2.4	.4	.1	.4	.2	0
Soybeans, dry	21.3	3.1	4.4	12.3	1.6	0
Nuts and Seeds	g	g	g	g	g	mg
Beechnuts, dried	50.0	5.7	21.9	20.1	1.7	0
Butternuts, dried	57.0	1.3	10.4	42.7	8.7	0
Chia seeds, dried	26.3	10.5	7.3	7.3	3.9	0
Hickory nuts, dried	64.4	7.0	32.6	21.9	1.0	0
Soybean kernels, roasted & toasted	24.0	3.2	5.6	12.7	1.5	0
Walnuts, black	56.6	3.6	12.7	37.5	3.3	0
Walnuts, English/ Persian	61.9	5.6	14.2	39.1	6.8	0
Pork	g	g	g	g	g	mg
Pork, cured, bacon, raw	57.5	21.3	26.3	6.8	.8	67
Pork, cured, breakfast strips, raw	37.1	12.9	16.9	5.6	.9	69
Pork, cured, salt pork, raw	80.5	29.4	38.0	9.4	.7	86
Pork, fresh, ham, raw	20.8	7.5	9.7	2.2	.2	74

Omega-3 Fatty Acids and Other Fat Components in Selected Foods

Food item	Total fat	Total satu- rated	Total monoun- saturated	Total polyun- saturated	Total Omega-3	Cholesterol
Pork, fresh, jowl, raw	69.6	25.3	32.9	8.1	.6	90
Pork, fresh, leaf fat, raw	94.2	45.2	37.2	7.3	.9	110
Pork, fresh, separable fat, raw	76.7	27.9	35.7	8.2	.7	93
Poultry	g	g	g	g	g	mg
Chicken, broiler fryers, flesh & skin, giblets, neck, raw	14.8	4.2	6.1	3.2	.1	90
Chicken, dark meat, w/o skin, raw	4.3	1.1	1.3	1.0	Tr	80
Chicken, light meat, w/o skin, raw	1.7	.4	.4	.4	Tr	58
Chicken, skin only, raw	32.4	9.1	13.5	6.8	.3	109
Turkey, flesh, with skin, roasted	9.7	2.8	3.2	2.5	.1	82
Vegetables	g	g	g	g	g	mg
Beans, Navy, sprouted, cooked	.8	Tr	Tr	.5	.3	0
Bean, pinto, sprouted, cooked	.9	.1	Tr	.5	.3	0
Broccoli, raw	.4	Tr	Tr	.2	.1	0
Cauliflower, raw	.2	Tr	Tr	Tr	.1	0
Kale, raw	.7	Tr	Tr	.3	.2	0
Leeks, freeze-dried, raw	2.1	.3	Tr	1.2	.7	0
Lettuce, butterhead, raw	.2	Tr	Tr	.1	.1	0
Radish seeds, sprouted, raw	2.5	.7	.4	1.1	.7	0
Seaweed, Spirulina, dried	7.7	2.6	.7	2.0	.8	0
Soybeans, green, raw	6.8	.7	.8	3.8	3.2	0
Soybeans, mature seeds, sprouted, cooked	4.5	.5	.5	2.5	2.1	0
Spinach, raw	.4	Tr	Tr	.1	.1	0
Finfish	g	g	g	g	g	mg
Anchovy, European	4.8	1.3	1.2	1.6	1.4	—
Bass, freshwater	2.0	.4	.7	.7	.3	59
Bass, striped	2.3	.5	.7	.8	.8	80
Bluefish	6.5	1.4	2.9	1.6	1.2	59
Burbot	.8	.2	.1	.3	.2	60

Food item	Total fat	Total satu- rated	Total monoun- saturated	Total polyun- saturated	Total Omega-3	Cholesterol
Capelin	8.2	1.5	3.8	1.5	1.2	—
Carp	5.6	1.1	2.3	1.4	.6	67
Catfish, brown bullhead	2.7	.6	1.0	.8	.5	75
Catfish, channel	4.3	1.0	1.6	1.0	.3	58
Cisco	1.9	.4	.5	.6	.5	—
Cod, Atlantic	.7	.1	.1	.3	.3	43
Cod, Pacific	.6	.1	.1	.2	.2	37
Croaker, Atlantic	3.2	1.1	1.2	.5	.2	61
Dogfish, spiny	10.2	2.2	4.2	2.7	2.0	52
Dolphinfish	.7	.2	.1	.2	.1	—
Drum, black	2.5	.7	.8	.5	.2	—
Drum, freshwater	4.9	1.1	2.2	1.2	.6	64
Eel, European	18.8	3.5	10.9	1.4	.9	108
Flounder, unspecified	1.0	.2	.3	.3	.2	46
Flounder, yellowtail	1.2	.3	.2	.3	.2	—
Grouper, jewfish	1.3	.3	.3	.4	.3	49
Grouper, red	.8	.2	.1	.2	.2	—
Haddock	.7	.1	.1	.2	.2	63
Hake, Atlantic	.6	.2	.2	.1	Tr	—
Hake, Pacific	1.6	.3	.3	.6	.4	—
Hake, red	.9	.2	.3	.3	.2	—
Hake, silver	2.6	.5	.7	.9	.6	—
Hake, unspecified	1.9	.5	.6	.5	.5	—
Halibut, Greenland	13.8	2.4	8.4	1.4	.9	46
Halibut, Pacific	2.3	.3	.8	.7	.5	32
Herring, Atlantic	9.0	2.0	3.7	2.1	1.7	60
Herring, Pacific	13.9	3.3	6.9	2.4	1.8	77
Herring, round	4.4	1.3	.8	1.5	1.3	28
Mackerel, Atlantic	13.9	3.6	5.4	3.7	2.6	80
Mackerel, chub	11.5	3.0	4.7	3.0	2.2	52
Mackerel, horse	4.1	1.2	1.4	.9	.6	41
Mackerel, Japanese horse	7.8	2.5	2.4	2.3	1.9	48
Mackerel, king	13.0	2.5	5.9	3.2	2.2	53
Mullet, striped	3.7	1.2	1.1	1.1	.6	49
Mullet, unspecified	4.4	.3	1.3	1.5	1.1	34
Ocean perch	1.6	.3	.6	.5	.2	42
Perch, white	2.5	.6	.9	.7	.4	80
Perch, yellow	.9	.2	.1	.4	.3	90
Pike, northern	.7	.1	.2	.2	.1	39
Pike, walleye	1.2	.2	.3	.4	.3	86
Plaice, European	1.5	.3	.5	.4	.2	70
Pollock	1.0	.1	.1	.5	.5	71
Pompano, Florida	9.5	3.5	2.6	1.1	.6	50

Omega-3 Fatty Acids and Other Fat Components in Selected Foods

Food item	Total fat	Total saturated	Total monounsaturated	Total polyunsaturated	Total Omega-3	Cholesterol
Ratfish	1.2	.3	.4	.1	.1	—
Rockfish, brown	3.3	.8	.8	1.0	.7	—
Rockfish, canary	1.8	.4	.5	.6	.5	34
Rockfish, unspecified	1.4	.2	.3	.6	.5	—
Sablefish	15.3	3.2	8.1	2.0	1.5	49
Salmon, Atlantic	5.4	.8	1.8	2.1	1.4	—
Salmon, chinook	10.4	2.5	4.5	2.1	1.5	—
Salmon, chum	6.6	1.5	2.9	1.5	1.1	74
Salmon, coho	6.0	1.1	2.1	1.7	1.0	—
Salmon, pink	3.4	.6	.9	1.4	1.0	—
Salmon, sockeye	8.6	1.5	4.1	1.9	1.3	—
Saury	9.2	1.6	4.8	1.8	1.4	19
Scad, Muroaji	8.7	2.8	2.2	2.6	2.1	47
Scad, other	.5	.1	.1	.1	Tr	27
Sea bass, Japanese	1.5	.4	.3	.5	.4	41
Seatrout, sand	2.3	.7	.8	.4	.3	—
Seatrout, spotted	1.7	.5	.4	.3	.2	—
Shark, unspecified	1.9	.3	.4	.8	.5	44
Sheepshead	2.4	.6	.7	.5	.2	—
Smelt, pond	.7	.2	.1	.3	.3	72
Smelt, rainbow	2.6	.5	.7	.9	.8	70
Smelt, sweet	4.6	1.6	1.2	1.0	.6	25
Snapper, red	1.2	.2	.2	.4	.2	—
Sole, European	1.2	.3	.4	.2	.1	50
Sprat	5.8	1.4	2.0	1.5	1.3	38
Sturgeon, Atlantic	6.0	1.2	1.7	2.1	1.5	—
Sturgeon, common	3.3	.8	1.6	.5	.4	—
Sunfish, pumpkinseed	.7	.1	.1	.2	.1	67
Swordfish	2.1	.6	.8	.2	.2	39
Trout, Arctic char	7.7	1.6	4.6	.9	.6	—
Trout, brook	2.7	.7	.8	.9	.6	68
Trout, lake	9.7	1.7	3.6	3.4	2.0	48
Trout, rainbow	3.4	.6	1.0	1.2	.6	57
Tuna, albacore	4.9	1.2	1.2	1.8	1.5	54
Tuna, bluefin	6.6	1.7	2.2	2.0	1.6	38
Tuna, skipjack	1.9	.7	.4	.6	.4	47
Tuna, unspecified	2.5	.9	.6	.5	.5	—
Whitefish, lake	6.0	.9	2.0	2.2	1.5	60
Whiting, European	.5	.1	.1	.1	.1	31
Wolffish, Atlantic	2.4	.4	.8	.8	.6	—
Crustaceans	g	g	g	g	g	mg
Crab, Alaska king	.8	.1	.1	.3	.3	—
Crab, blue	1.3	.2	.2	.5	.4	78

Food item	Total fat	Total satu-rated	Total monoun-saturated	Total polyun-saturated	Total Omega-3	Cholesterol
Crab, Dungeness	1.0	.1	.2	.3	.5	59
Crab, queen	1.1	.1	.2	.4	.3	127
Crayfish, unspecified	1.4	.3	.4	.3	.1	158
Lobster, European	.8	.1	.2	.2	.2	129
Lobster, northern	.9	.2	.2	.2	.2	95
Shrimp, Atlantic brown	1.5	.3	.3	.5	.3	142
Shrimp, Atlantic white	1.5	.2	.2	.6	.4	182
Shrimp, Japanese (kuruma) prawn	2.5	.5	.5	1.0	.5	58
Shrimp, northern	1.5	.2	.3	.6	.5	125
Shrimp, other	1.3	.4	.3	.3	.2	128
Shrimp, unspecified	1.1	.2	.1	.4	.3	147
Spiny lobster, Caribbean	1.4	.2	.2	.6	.3	140
Spiny lobster, southern rock	1.0	.1	.2	.3	.3	—
Mollusks	**g**	**g**	**g**	**g**	**g**	**mg**
Abalone, New Zealand	1.0	.2	.2	.2	Tr	—
Abalone, South African	1.1	.3	.3	.2	Tr	—
Clam, hardshell	.6	Tr	Tr	.1	Tr	31
Clam, hen	.7	.2	.1	.1	Tr	—
Clam, littleneck	.8	.1	.1	.1	Tr	—
Clam, Japanese hardshell	.8	.1	.1	.2	.2	—
Clam, softshell	2.0	.3	.2	.6	.4	—
Clam, surf	.8	.1	.1	.2	.2	—
Conch, unspecified	2.7	.6	.5	1.1	1.0	141
Cuttlefish, unspecified	.6	.1	.1	.1	Tr	—
Mussel, blue	2.2	.4	.5	.6	.5	38
Mussel, Mediterranean	1.5	.4	.4	.3	.2	—
Octopus, common	1.0	.3	.1	.3	.2	—
Oyster, eastern	2.5	.6	.2	.7	.4	47
Oyster, European	2.0	.4	.2	.7	.6	30
Oyster, Pacific	2.3	.5	.4	.9	.6	—
Periwinkle, common	3.3	.6	.6	1.1	.7	101
Scallop, Atlantic deep-sea	.8	.1	.1	.3	.2	37
Scallop, calico	.7	.1	—	.2	.2	—
Scallop, unspecified	.8	.1	.1	.3	.2	45
Squid, Atlantic	1.2	.3	.1	.5	.4	—
Squid, short-finned	2.0	.4	.4	.7	.6	—
Squid, unspecified	1.1	.3	.1	.4	.3	—

Omega-3 Fatty Acids and Other Fat Components in Selected Fooods

Food item	Total fat	Total satu- rated	Total monoun- saturated	Total polyun- saturated	Total Omega-3	Cholesterol
Fish Oils	g	g	g	g	g	mg
Cod liver oil	100	17.6	51.2	25.8	19.2	570
Herring oil	100	19.2	60.3	16.1	12.07	766
Menhaden oil	100	33.6	32.5	29.5	21.71	521
MaxEPA™, concentrated fish body oils	100	25.4	28.3	41.1	29.4	600
Salmon oil	100	23.8	39.7	29.9	20.9	485

Selected References

Albrink, M.L., Ullrich, I.H., Blehschmidt, N.G., Mike, P., Rogers, J.S. "The Beneficial Effect of Fish Oil Supplements on Serum Lipids and Clotting Function of Patients with Type II Diabetes Mellitus." Paper presented at the American Diabetes Association Scientific Seminar, Anaheim, California, June, 1986.

Altschule, F.A. "A Tale of Two Lipids: Cholesterol and Eicosapentaenoic Acid." *Chest* 89(1986): 601–2.

Ballard-Barbash, R., Callaway, C.W. "Marine Fish Oils: Role in Prevention of Coronary Artery Disease." *Mayo Clinic Proceedings* 62(1987): 113–7.

Bang, H.O., Dyerberg, J. "Fish Consumption and Mortality From Coronary Heart Disease." *New England Journal of Medicine* 313(1985): 822–3.

Bang, H.O., Dyerberg, J., Brondum Nielsen, A. "Plasma Lipid and Lipoprotein Pattern in Greenlandic West-Coast Eskimos." *Lancet* 1(1971): 1143–6.

Bang, H.O., Dyerberg, J., Sinclair, H.M. "The Composition of the Eskimo Food in Northwestern Greenland." *American Journal of Clinical Nutrition* 33(1980): 2657–61.

Bronsgeest-Schoute, H.C., Gent, C.M. van, Luten, J.B., Ruiter, A. "The Effect of Various Intakes of Omega-3 Fatty Acids on the Blood Lipid Composition in Healthy Human Subjects." *American Journal of Clinical Nutrition* 34(1981): 1752–7.

Cartwright, I.J., Pockley, A.G., Galloway, J.H., Greaves, M., Preston, F.E. "The Effects of Dietary Omega-3 Polyunsaturated Fatty Acids on Erythrocyte Membrane Phospholipids, Eryocyte Deformability and Blood Viscosity in Healthy Volunteers." *Atherosclerosis* 55(1985): 267–81.

Connor, W.E. "Dietary Omega-3 Fatty Acid Deficiency and Visual Loss: Evidence for a Specific Nutritional Requirement." Paper presented at the Twentieth Joint Conference on Malnutrition of the U.S.-Japan Cooperative Medical Sciences Program, Bethesda, Maryland, July 15–17, 1985.

Selected References

Dyerberg, J., Bang, H.O. "Haemostatic Function and Platelet Polyunsaturated Acids in Eskimos." *Lancet* 2(1979): 433–5.

Dyerberg, J., Bang, H.O., Hjorne, N. "Plasma Cholesterol Concentrations in Caucasian Danes and Greenland West-Coast Eskimos," *Danish Medical Bulletin*, 24(1977): 52–5.

Dyerberg, J., Bang, H.O. Stoffersen, E., Moncada, S., Vane, J.R. "Eicosapentaenoic Acid and Prevention of Thrombosis and Atherosclerosis." *Lancet* 2(1978): 117–9.

Dyerberg, J., Mortensen, J.Z., Nielsen, H.H., Schmidt, E.B. "Omega-3 Polyunsaturated Fatty Acids and Ischaemic Heart Disease." *Lancet* 2(1982): 614.

Exler, J., Weihrauch, J.L. "Finfish: Comprehensive Evaluation of Fatty Acids in Foods." *Journal of the American Dietary Association* 69(1976): 243–8.

Fehily, A.M., Burr, M.L., Phillips, K.M., Deadman, N.M. "The Effect of Fatty Fish on Plasma Lipids and Lipoprotein Concentrations." *American Journal of Clinical Nutrition* 38(1983): 349–51.

Galloway, J.H., Cartwright, I.J., Woodcock, B.E. "Effects of Dietary Fish Oil Supplementation on the Fatty Acid Composition of the Human Platelet Membrane: Demonstration of Selectivity in the Incorporation of Eicosapentaenoic Acid into Membrane Phospholipid Pools." *Clinical Science* 68(1985): 449–54.

Glomset, J.A. "Fish, Fatty Acids and Human Health." *New England Journal of Medicine* 312(1985): 1253–4.

Green, D., Barreres, L., Borensztajn, J., Kaplan, P., Reddy, M.N., Rovner, R., Simon, H. "A Double-Blind, Placebo-Controlled Trial of Fish Oil Concentrate in Stroke Patients." *Stroke* 16(1985): 706–9.

Goodnight, S.H. Jr., Harris, W.S., Connor, W.E. "The Effects of Dietary Omega-3 Fatty Acids on Platelet Composition and Function in Man: A Prospective, Controlled Study." *Blood* 58(1981): 880–5.

Goodnight, S.H. Jr., Harris, W.S., Connor, W.E., Illingworth, D.R. "Polyunsaturated Fatty Acids, Hyperlipidemia and Thrombosis." *Atherosclerosis* 2(1982): 87–113.

Harris, W.S. "Health Effects of Omega-3 Fatty Acids." *Contemporary Nutrition* 10(1985): 1–2.

Harris, W.S., Connor, W.E., Inkeles, S.B., Illingworth, D.R. "Dietary Omega-3 Fatty Acids Prevent Carbohydrate Induced Hypertriglyceridemia." *Metabolism* 33(1984): 1016–9.

Harris, W.S., Connor, W.E., McMurry, M.P. "The Comparative Reductions of the Plasma Lipids and Lipoproteins by Dietary Polyunsaturated Fats: Salmon Oil Versus Vegetable Oils." *Metabolism* 32(1983): 179–84.

Hartog, C. den, Schaik, Th.F.S.M. van, Dalderup, L.M., Drion, E.F., Mulder, T. "The Diet of Volunteers Participating in a Long Term Epidemiological Field Survey on Coronary Heart Disease at Zutphen, the Netherlands." *Voeding* 26(1965): 184–208.

Herold, P.M., Kinsella, J.E. "Fish Oil Consumption and Decreased Risk of Cardiovascular Disease: A Comparison of Findings From Animal and Human Feeding Trials." *American Journal of Clinical Nutrition* 43(1986): 566–98.

Hirai, A., Hamazaki, T., Terano, T., Nishikawa, T., Tamura, Y., Kumagai, A., Sajiki, J. "Eicosapentaenoic Acid and Platelet Function in Japanese." *Lancet* 2(1980): 1132–3.

Hornstra, G., Hadderman, F., Hoor, F. "Fish Oils, Prostaglandin and Arterial Thrombosis." *Lancet* 2(1979): 1080.

Houtsmuller, A.J., Hal-ferwerda, J. Van, Zahn, K.J., Henkes, H.E. "Favorable Influences of Linoleic Acid on the Progression of Diabetic Micro- and Macroangiopathy." *Nutrition and Metabolism* 24(1980): 105.

Hulley, S.B., Rosenman, R.H., Bawol, R.D., Brand, R.J. "Epidemiology as a Guide to Clinical Decisions: The Association Between Triglyceride and Coronary Heart Disease." *New England Journal of Medicine* 302(1980): 1383–9.

Kagawa, Y., Nishizawa, M., Suzuki, M. "Eicosapolyenoic Acid of Serum Lipids of Japanese Islanders with Low Incidence of Cardiovascular Diseases." *Journal of Nutritional Science Vitaminol* 28(1982): 441–53.

Kamada, T., Yamashita, T., Baba, Y., Kai, M., Setoyama, S., Chuman, Y., Otsuji, S. "Dietary Sardine Oil Increases Erythrocyte Membrane Fluidity in Diabetic Patients." *Diabetes* 35(1986): 604–11.

Kannel, W.B., Castelli, W.P., Gordon, T., McNamara, P.M. "Serum Cholesterol Lipoproteins and the Risk of Coronary Heart Disease." *Annals of Internal Medicine* 74(1971): 1–12.

Karmali, R.A., Marsh, J., Fuchs, C. "Effect of Omega-3 Fatty Acids on Growth of a Rat Mammary Tumor." *Journal of the National Cancer Institute* 73(1984): 457.

Keys, A., *Seven Countries: A Multivariate Analysis of Death and Coronary Heart Disease*. Cambridge, Mass.: Harvard University Press, 1980.

Keys, A., Aravanis, C., Blackburn, H.W., et al. "Epidemiological Studies Related to Coronary Heart Disease: Characteristics of Men Aged 40–59 in Seven Countries." *Acta Medica Scandinavia* (1967): 460.

Kinsella, J.E. "Food Components with Potential Therapeutic Benefits: The Omega-3 Polyunsaturated Fatty Acids of Fish Oils." *Food Technology* (1986): 89–98.

Kromhout, D., Bosschieter, E.B., de Lezenne Coulander, C. "The Inverse Relation Between Fish Consumption and a 20-Year Mortality From Coronary Heart Disease." *New England Journal of Medicine* 312(1985): 1205–9.

Lands, W.E.M., *Fish and Human Health*, Orlando, Florida: Academic Press, 1986.

Lee, T.H., Hoover, R.L., Williams, J.D. "Effect of Dietary Enrichment with Eicosapentaenoic and Docosahexaenoic Acids on In Vitro Neutrophil and Monocyte Leukotriene Generation and Neutrophil Function." *New England Journal of Medicine* 312(1985) 1217–24.

Lossonczy, T.O. von, Ruiter, A., Bronsgeest-Schoute, H.C., Gent, C.V.M. van, Hermus, R.J.J. "The Effect of a Fish Diet on Serum Lipids in Healthy Human Subjects." *American Journal of Clinical Nutrition* 31(1978): 1340–6.

312(1985) 1217–24.

Lowering the Risk of Coronary Heart Disease Through Nutritional Intervention: The Possible Role of Omega-3 Fatty Acids, *Symposium Sponsored by The Department of Preventive Medicine and Clinical Epidemiology, Harvard Medical School,* 1986: The New York Academy of Sciences.

Monro, J., Carini, C., Brostoff, J. "Migraine Is a Food-Allergic Disease." *Lancet* (1984): 719–21.

Monta, I., Saito, Y., Chang, W.C., Murota, S. "Effects of Purified Eicosapentaenoic Acid on Arachidonic Acid Metabolism in Cultured Murine Aortic Smooth Muscle Cells, Vessel Walls and Platelets." *Lipids* 18(1983): 42–9.

Nestel, P.J., Connor, W.E., Reardon, M.F., Connor, S., Wong, S. Boston, R. "Suppression by Diets Rich in Fish Oil of Very Low Density Lipoprotein Production in Man." *Journal of Clinical Investigation* 74(1984): 82–9.

Phillipson, B.E., Rothrock, D.W., Connor, W.E., Harris, W.E., Illingworth, D.R. "Reduction of Plasma Lipids, Lipoproteins and Apoproteins by Dietary Fish Oil in Patients with Hypertriglyceridemia." *New England Journal of Medicine* 312(1985): 1210–6.

Prescott, S.M. "The Effect of Eicosapentaenoic Acid on Leukotriene B Production by Human Neutrophils." *Journal of Biologic Chemistry* 259(1984): 7615–21.

Sanders, T.A.B., Naismith, D.J., Haines, A.P., Vickers, M. "Cod-liver Oil, Platelet Fatty Acids and Bleeding Time." *Lancet* 1(1980): 1189.

Sanders, T.A.B., Vickers, M., Haines, A.P. "Effect on Blood Lipids and Haemostasis of a Supplement of Cod-Liver Oil Rich in Eicosapentaenoic and Docosahexaenoic Acids, in Healthy Young Men." *Clinical Science* 61(1981): 317–24.

Saynor, R., Verel, D., Gillott, T. "The Long Term Effect of Dietary Supplementation With Fish Lipid Concentrate on Serum Lipids, Bleeding Time, Platelets and Angina."*Atherosclerosis* 50(1984): 3–10.

Schacky, C. von, Fischer, S., Weber, P.C. "Long-Term Effects of Dietary Marine omega-3 Fatty Acids Upon Plasma and Cellular Lipids, Platelet Function and Eicosanoid Formation in Humans." *Journal of Clinical Investigation* 76(1985): 1626–31.

Seiss, W., Scherer, B., Böhlig, B., Roth, P., Kurzmann, I., Weber, P.C. "Platelet Membrane Fatty Acids, Platelet Aggregation and Thromboxane Formation During A Mackerel Diet." *Lancet* 1(1980): 441–4.

Stansby, M.E. "Nutritional Properties of Fish Oils." *World Review of Nutritional Diet* 11(1969): 46–105.

Teas, J., Harbison, M.L., Gelman, R.S. "Dietary Seaweed as a Protective Factor in DMBA-Induced Mammary Carcinogenesis." Paper presented at the International Breast Cancer Research Conference, Denver, Colorado, abstract 53, 1983.

Terano, T., Hirai, A., Hamazaki, T. "Effect of Oral Administration of Highly Purified Eicosapentaenoic Acid on Platelet Function, Blood Viscosity and Cell Deformability in Healthy Human Subjects." *Atherosclerosis* 46(1983): 321–31.

Thorngren, M., Gustafson, A. "Effects of 11-Week Increase in Dietary Eicosapentaenoic Acid on Bleeding Time, Lipids and Platelet Aggregation." *Lancet* 2(1981): 1190–3.

Turkowski, J.J., Cave, W.T. "Dietary Effects of Menhaden Oil on Rat Mammary Tumors." *Journal of the National Cancer Institute* 74(1985): 1145.

Willis, A.L. "Nutritional and Pharmacological Factors in Eicosanoid Biology." *Nutritional Review* 39(1981): 289–301.